Caring for the Under-8s

Working to achieve good practice

Jennie and Lance Lindon

Foreword by Gillian Pugh

150th YEAR

M

MACMILLAN

To our children – Drew and Tanith

We are grateful to everyone who offered constructive criticism of early drafts of the book, in particular Valerie Farebrother, Jan Mallam, Terry Smyth, Stuart Sillars, Emma Lee, and Maureen Smith. The final draft benefited from Andrew Nash's careful editing.

We value our contact with many early years workers. We especially acknowledge helpful and invigorating discussions with members of the Early Childhood Unit of the National Children's Bureau.

We wish to thank the staff, parents and children of Ravenstone School, South London for permission to use photographs taken during the school day and for the illustration on page 122. All the photographs were taken by Lance Lindon. The original drawings for the cartoons were produced by Tanith and Drew Lindon.

All the examples describing children, early years workers and centres for the under-8s are taken from the experience of real people and places. We have changed names and a few other details to maintain confidentiality.

First published 1993 by
THE MACMILLAN PRESS LTD
Houndmills, Basingstoke, Hampshire RG21 2XS
and London
Companies and representatives
throughout the world

ISBN 0–333–57424–9

A catalogue record for this book is available from the British Library

Filmset by Wearset, Boldon, Tyne and Wear
Printed in Hong Kong

10 9 8 7 6 5 4 3 2 1
02 01 00 99 98 97 96 95 94 93

Contents

Foreword   v

About this book   vi

1 Children and their development   1
   1.1 What happens in childhood   1
   1.2 What do children need?   5
   1.3 How do children develop?   8
   1.4 Recognising children as individuals   12

2 Good practice with the under-8s   18
   2.1 Principles and good practice   18
   2.2 Good practice and the law   22
   2.3 Equal opportunities   24
   2.4 Partnership with parents   27
   2.5 Organising children's environment   34
   2.6 Planning what to do with children   39
   2.7 Observation, assessment and record-keeping   44

3 Physical and emotional well-being of children   55
   3.1 Keeping babies and children well and healthy   55
   3.2 A healthy diet   59
   3.3 Teaching children to look after themselves   65
   3.4 Infections and special health needs   73
   3.5 Helping children in distress   81

4 Physical development   86
   4.1 Children's physical development 0–7   86
   4.2 Enjoyable and safe activities for children   94

5 The development of communication   101
   5.1 Learning to communicate   101
   5.2 How you can help   107
   5.3 Learning to read and write   119

6 The development of thinking   125
   6.1 Can you look through children's eyes?   125

6.2   How you can help – early maths and science   130
6.3   How you can help – ideas about people and growing up   138

7   Children's behaviour and adults' behaviour   142

7.1   Why do children behave as they do?   142
7.2   Making sense of what is going on   145
7.3   Clear rules and consequences   149
7.4   Tactics to avoid   155

Final thoughts   161

Appendix 1: NVQs/SVQs   163

Appendix 2: How to find out more   164

Appendix 3: Useful books and articles   166

Index   167

Foreword

The early years of a child's life are of critical and lasting importance. We now know that a high percentage of children's learning takes place in the first five years, and that this is the time when attitudes are formed, when first relationships are made, when concepts are developed, and when the foundation for all skills and later learning are laid.

The adults who care for children during these early years – whether as parents, grandparents or friends, or as childminders, nannies, or playgroup or nursery workers – therefore find themselves in an important and responsible position, as they seek to observe, understand and respond to the needs of children.

Caring for the Under-8s is primarily intended for those who are already working with, or who are intending to work with, young children. Two important recent developments make its publication particularly timely: the 1989 Children Act, which emphasises the importance of good-quality care for children under 8 and the need for well-trained workers; and the introduction of National Vocational Qualifications and Scottish Vocational Qualifications, which provide a national framework for assessing and accrediting workers in the care and education of young children.

Understanding how children develop is the starting point for child-care workers knowing that each child is unique in his or her own individual likes and dislikes, abilities, behaviour, temperament and family circumstances, but is growing up within a common developmental framework. But good-quality care goes far beyong this, requiring commitment to a value base that respects individuals and promotes equality of opportunity for all children; and attitudes and skills to respond appropriately to children and their parents, caring and nurturing and extending children's learning, working in partnership with parents.

Caring for the Under-8s provides support for all these aspects of quality child care. Based on research and good practice, it includes the underpinning knowledge that students require, but also contains practical activities and case studies to encourage them to reflect on and develop their own practice. It will be an invaluable resource for students, child-care workers and tutors alike.

Gillian Pugh
Director
Early Childhood Unit
National Children's Bureau

About this book

Caring for young children is an important and valuable job. The work carries great responsibility, but that doesn't stop it being both very enjoyable and satisfying.

Caring for the under-8s offers a wide range of job opportunities. You can work with a team in day nurseries, children's centres, family centres, playgroups or schools. Or you can be an individual worker as a nanny or childminder.

This book provides information and support that will help you to care for children up to the age of 8 in an effective and creative way, whatever the setting in which you are offering this care.

Who is this book for?

This book will be useful to you if you are already working with the under-8s in a paid job or as a volunteer. It will also be useful if you are training or planning to train for this work.

If you are already working with young children you will find that the book will build on your existing skills and knowledge. It will help you prepare for a National or Scottish Vocational Qualification (NVQ/SVQ) in child care and education, up to and including Level 3.

If you are a student or trainee taking a BTEC, City & Guilds, RSA or NNEB course including a General National Vocational Qualification (GNVQ) in health and social care at Level 3, you will find that the book covers what you need to know about child care and development.

Much of the book is also relevant to work in a residential home for children or in a hospital working with children who are sick. Parents may also find information and help which will reinforce and build on what they already know in practice.

Why under-8s?

We have followed the NVQ/SVQ framework of covering the care and development of children up to their 8th birthday. The tradition of talking about under-5s and over-5s has come from the statutory age for starting school in the UK. Of course, the 8th birthday is no more magical a watershed than is the 5th.

However, qualifications such as those of the NNEB, which set out to equip workers for both care and education settings, already cover the early years of middle childhood. The Children Act 1989 legislated for minimum standards in child care for children under 8 years.

It is not that 8-year-olds are suddenly independent of all need for care. They are, however, much more able to attend to many of their own physical needs. They are learning skills of literacy and numeracy which enable them to direct some of their own learning. They need a different kind of care.

The aims of the book

We hope that this book will help you in achieving good practice in caring for the under-8s, whatever the circumstances in which you are working. We hope that it will help you to feel more confident in your work and more able to explain what you do and why.

Information about child development is given in ways which should help you to think about your work from a new point of view. We have included many practical activities, examples and case studies to help extend your skills in working with young children and their parents.

How to use this book

You can use this book on your own or with a supervisor. It is written in seven main chapters, each covering a particular area of child care and development. The sections can be used in the order that suits your own needs.

If you have a tutor or supervisor, you can plan your study together, deciding which sections to work on at a particular time. You can then build up a programme of learning to make sure that you get the most out of your work experience. At the end of the book you will find details of the links between this book and the NVQ/SVQ qualifications in child care and education.

Most of the activities can be done on their own, without help. Others will first need to be discussed and agreed with a workplace supervisor. Even if you work alone, we suggest that you discuss your work with a colleague or tutor, or with someone who works in a similar care setting to your own.

You will get more out of the book if you take any available opportunities to discuss your work. Of course, you must be careful not to break confidentiality regarding information and personal details about individual children, families or colleagues.

Most of the activities encourage you to reflect on your experience, to analyse what happened and to try to make sense of it. These skills are needed in work with children and their families. The willingness to think and reflect is also crucial for any further study you may do. In caring for young children it is not enough simply to follow someone else's instructions. You need to *understand* what you are doing and to see how it relates to the children in your care.

We suggest that you develop the habit of keeping a written record of your learning. This may be required in some of the activities, or by your supervisor or tutor. Try always to keep a log or diary of your work experience. You should record what you felt at the time and how you were able at a later date to make sense of an event or experience, and what you learned.

Terms used

The word *worker* is used for anyone who is involved with children in the different settings. Workers and children can be male or female. So, the problem arises of whether to use 'he' or 'she' when writing about an individual. We have chosen either to address individual workers as 'you' – since 'you' are the readers of this book – or to refer to workers in the plural. Sometimes we write about children in general. When we are describing individual children, we have rung the changes between 'she' or 'he'. It will be obvious when we wish to make a point specifically about boys or girls, men or women.

We use the word *parent* to cover any man or woman who has parental responsibility for a child. We recognise that some adults who take this responsibility are not the biological parents.

We have used the word *race* to describe how one group of children and adults differs from another because of physical characteristics, such as skin colour and a shared cultural and traditional heritage. We are not entirely happy about using this word, especially since in the past the term 'race' has been associated with questionable claims about genetic differences. However, terms that have been used as an alternative – including 'ethnic group' and 'culture' – are sometimes misused to refer only to groups who are not white: they should be a way of describing anyone.

Occasionally we have used the words *white* or *black*, recognising that these are social labels rather than an accurate description of how children or adults look.

We use the phrase *children with disabilities* rather than *disabled children*. The former phrase gives the important message that we are talking first and foremost about children. We recognise the wide range of kinds of disability and different levels of severity that are covered by these words. Children with disabilities have the same needs as all children: their special needs are in addition.

In a few cases organisations are referred to by abbreviations or acronyms: these are explained in Appendix 2.

Information and advice

There are many practical suggestions in this workbook. However, you will have to make final decisions about using ideas in your particular setting and with the individual children in your care.

On some topics, for example medical conditions, we have summarised *briefly* the advice available at the time of writing. You might well need more information and would be wise to check that advice has not changed. For this reason we often suggest organisations for you to contact.

The information on publications and addresses of organisations is correct to our knowledge. However, books come into and go out of print; organisations change location. Sometimes we tell you the name of an organisation that has published books or leaflets: contact the organisation for the current cost and availability of publications – addresses and telephone numbers are given within the section or in Appendix 2.

The context

We have written *Caring for the Under-8s* during 1992 and in England. This gives a context of time and place to what we write. It is inevitable that we ourselves hold views about what is important and how workers should foster good practice with babies and young children. These are not just our own ideas: as well as visiting centres for children, we spend a lot of time talking with other people and reading what they write. We have tried to make our assumptions clear so you can make sense of what we have written and our reasons for writing it.

We hope that you will enjoy the book. We are sure that it will make you think and will help you in your work with the under-8s.

1 Children and their development

Traditions vary around the world about how parents should raise babies and children. Even within a single culture you will not find families behaving in exactly the same way towards their children. So is it possible to say anything in general about children and the years we call childhood? We believe it is: below are some important themes that are common for all children.

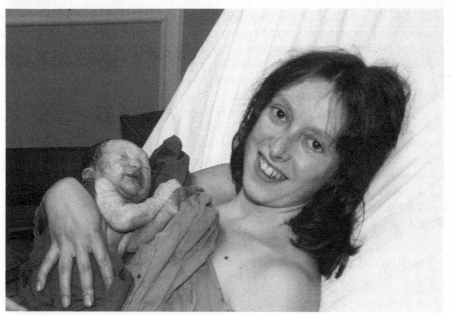

The first minutes of life outside the womb

Childhood is a time of change

It is inevitable that children themselves change as time passes. Even if the rest of their child's world stays fairly static, they themselves will change. They grow physically and their abilities extend; this in turn opens up other possibilities for them. Because individual babies and children keep changing, adults have to adjust in response.

Children in their turn react to changes that happen even in their small world. For example, many children around the world experience the readjustment that a new baby brings to a family and to their own life.

In many parts of the world children also make adjustments to settings outside their immediate family. For many the experience of some years in school will be a major cause for such adjustments. In many industrialised countries children make several changes in their early years, with attendance first at some kind of pre-school facility. Adults can help children with these transitions.

Experiences affect children

Individual experiences

What *happens* to children changes them in one way or another. They learn from their experiences. These may be as simple as the child realising that it hurts if she shuts her fingers in a drawer. But it can be more difficult to predict how a child will react to some events. Some children are angry over the arrival of a new baby, for instance; others are happy and excited, and for them these seem to be stronger emotions than jealousy.

Children's lives are altered by other changes in their family. Disruptions in family life – like having to go into hospital, or the death of a loved person – will distress children. However, such events do not inevitably cause long-term psychological problems: much depends on how the experience and the associated feelings are handled. Children seem to be more seriously disturbed by continued stress and upset than by single events.

Each experience gains meaning for children through how the important adults in their lives explain, or don't explain, the event. Words like 'divorce' only mean something to young children in the context of their own lives, whereas older children may have some idea based on the experiences of friends whose parents have divorced.

What matters most is how adults behave towards each other and to the children. Part of such behaviour is, of course, what parents, and other involved adults, *say*. Children need to be helped to understand what is likely to happen as a consequence of any change in family life. They need to be reassured, in a realistic way, about the stability of their own daily life.

H. Rudolph Schaffer came to the following conclusion in his review of research on children:

> . . . care needs to be taken about making sweeping generalizations and advancing global solutions. 'It all depends' may be an annoying phrase and it does not make good headlines, but it accurately reflects reality.
> H. Rudolph Schaffer 1990: *Making Decisions about Children*, p. 235
> (Basil Blackwell)

Social circumstances and prejudices

Children will be affected by the environment in which they are raised. This will reach them partly through the behaviour of their parents. Some circumstances can be very stressful for adults, for example serious money worries or living in unsafe conditions. Some parents may find it more difficult to raise children in a positive way that focuses on the children's needs.

Children of a racial or social group that is the butt of prejudice are at high risk of developing a poor self-image. Their families and other adults

Some things don't change . . .

who care for them may be able to strengthen their confidence against the prejudice, but it will remain a feature of the rest of their lives.

The experience of different generations

Successive generations of children share many similar experiences. However, some details of the environment do change from generation to generation.

The current generation of children has access to a level of technology that was scarcely predicted in their parents' childhood. In their grand-parents' early years it would have seemed like wild fantasy. Many children nowadays are at ease with calculators and computers. They watch television and video. You yourself may regret some consequences of children's comfort with this equipment, but focus on the positives as well.

Children need families

Children need to be cared for in their early years. They need people who care about them and what happens to them. The most usual way that this is managed, worldwide, is that children are raised in families. There are, however, many variations in how families look.

In the Britain of the 1990s the majority of children live with two parents. Yet just under a fifth of families are run by one parent without the permanent support of a partner; this is a fairly large minority. The vast majority of lone parents are women: only about ten per cent are men running families alone. Available statistics suggest that the number of families run by lone parents will increase.

Some families include step-parents and children from previous rela-tionships. Some have grandparents or other relatives as a permanent part of the family. In some families relatives other than parents take a lot of the responsibility for child care.

Children learn social values

Children learn from their families ways of behaving and ways of looking at the world. The values they learn may include religious beliefs as well as more general opinions about how other people should be treated. As they get

---

ACTIVITY

Advice to parents and others who care for young children has changed over the years, even within one cultural tradition. The children themselves are not likely to have changed, so what is going on?

1 Try to gather examples of advice given over the last thirty to forty years. You could track this down by:

- asking your own parents whether they used any books to help them raise you and, if so, whether they still have the books;
- looking out at jumble sales or secondhand bookshops for advice books more than 10–15 years old;
- getting hold of Christina Hardyment's *Dream Babies* (Jonathan Cape, 1983), which describes the differing

advice given to parents in the UK over a period of two hundred years.

Look out for any differences or similarities in the advice given.

Does a different picture emerge of what is or was considered normal for babies and young children, for example, in feeding or toilet-training?

2 What could your findings tell you about your current assumptions and the need to check them? (Do avoid the temptation to believe that anyone offering advice in the past was just wrong and that current advice is the final, unchanging statement of how to care well for children!)

older and make friends, they are influenced by a wider circle of contacts. Whatever the values held by their families, children will later encounter alternative views. Some of these will come from workers like yourself.

By the time they are 3 or 4 years old, children are aware of differences in skin colour. They work out that there are two sexes. They do not automatically believe that people of one colour or sex are better or worse than others. However, they may quickly accept and repeat prejudiced attitudes unless these are challenged.

Children who express racist or sexist attitudes towards other children or adults may clearly damage others. But they themselves are not developing a genuine sense of self-worth and confidence, since their positive view of themselves depends on denigrating others.

Reading on . . .

★ De'Ath, Erica 1991: *Changing Families – a guide for early years workers* (VOLCUF/National Stepfamily Association).
★ Konner, Melvin 1992: *Childhood* (Little, Brown & Co.).
★ Tobin, J. J., D. Wu and D. Davidson 1989: *Preschool in Three Cultures* (Yale University Press).

1.2 What do children need?

All children have physical, emotional and intellectual needs. Although these are universal there are different ways of meeting them. For example, you can meet a child's need for healthy eating by different ways of balancing a diet. Cultural traditions vary in how adults are expected to make sense of children's needs and to treat them.

The needs of children

Wherever you are working with children and whatever your job title, you need to approach each child as a rounded individual. Even if your place of work was set up to attend particularly to some of these needs rather than others, you should not forget the bigger picture of what children need. For instance, when children are sick and in hospital, they still need company and play.

Physical needs

All children share these physical needs:

- *Protection* – shelter and clothing that protect them appropriately for the climate.
- *Food and drink* – regular nutritious food and water that is safe to drink.
- *Care and hygiene* – physical care and a standard of hygiene that will keep them as healthy as possible.
- *Activity and rest* – a combination of varied games and activities, indoors and out, in a safe yet interesting environment, with sufficient sleep and rest.
- *Space* – sufficient space in which to move and play.

Meeting physical needs is basic to children's well-being. A child who is hungry or exhausted will be not able to enjoy your company or play with other children. A child who is physically well will have the energy to benefit from activities that you offer. She will also get bored if what you offer does not suit her needs.

Emotional needs

Children's emotional needs have to be met just as much as their physical needs. Children need all of the following:

- *Attention* – that is physically close and that communicates warmth and caring.
- *Concern* – consideration for their wants and interests.
- *Security* – the sense of belonging and of being accepted for themselves.
- *Companionship* – the happy company of adults and other children.
- *Continuity and stimulus* – some predictability in their everyday life, with new experiences that provide interest.
- *Support and affirmation* – guidance through encouragement and praise more often than control through punishment.

Children can appreciate a quiet atmosphere

- *Boundaries* – clear limits for acceptable behaviour, set by adults and consistently applied.

Intellectual needs

Children are continually learning new ideas and taking in new information. To grow intellectually, children need everything mentioned already for their physical and emotional needs. They also need the following experiences:

- *Freedom to learn* – opportunities to learn from different experiences and to discover some things for themselves.
- *Freedom to make mistakes* – opportunities to make mistakes without being made to feel stupid.
- *Support* – adults who support, encourage and teach them.
- *Increasing independence* – chances to grow in independence through progressively taking on more responsibility and being trusted with tasks.
- *Information* – and a framework in which to make sense of their growing knowledge.
- *Freedom to explore* – opportunities to explore ideas through talk with other children and adults.

Children with special needs

Some children have individual needs which are special to them. Such needs are *in addition to* those just listed: they are not instead of them.

Others' use of the term 'children with special needs' tells you a lot about what they judge to be normal or usual. We would not, for example, use 'special needs' to describe the hair- or skin-care needs of black children – these are very ordinary, everyday needs. They only seem 'special' to white workers who work largely with white children.

Children with disabilities may need special attention if their disability affects how they can communicate, move about or make use of play materials. Again, the extent to which these needs seem special depends a lot on the development of the other children and how the play environment is organised.

Strictly speaking, 'special needs' also refers to children whose development is very much in advance of their peers. Such children, sometimes called 'gifted', can become very frustrated in an environment and with a programme of activities that fail to stretch them according to their abilities.

Children's need to play

Children around the world need and deserve the opportunity to play. However, you will see many differences between and within cultures on how adults view children's play. You yourself may have experienced people who all but dismiss your job on the grounds that it must be easy since it's just playing about with children.

In order to play, children need the following.

Playtime

Children's play is not the same as adult leisure time. For children, play can absorb much of their waking life. It is the way in which they learn. In some ways children's play is their work: this is the reason that they take their games so seriously. Children will view involvement in some adult activities as a form of play. However, children cannot play if they are forced to work at jobs in an adult world. Long hours and exhausting work make up life for many children in some countries.

Playmates

Although children sometimes enjoy quiet solitary play, they also want the opportunity to play with someone else – adult or child. Children do not want to be told always to 'go and play': they also want the invitation to 'come and play with me'.

Playthings

Children will convert all sorts of objects into playthings. They do not need bought and manufactured toys, although this is the source of many playthings for children in the industrialised countries. If you think back to your childhood, you may remember that some of your most absorbing games involved dressing up in adult cast-offs or building camps out of junk material.

ACTIVITY

Please read the following excerpt and then think about it with the help of the questions that follow.

From the 'Geographica' section, *National Geographic*, June 1992:

> Researchers long thought that African Pygmy children grew much as other children do until they failed to have an adolescent growth spurt. A study of Zaire's Efe . . . shows, however, that the typical child . . . starts out smaller and falls further and further behind on the growth chart in the first five years of life.
>
> Preliminary results of the study, by Robert C. Bailey of the University of California, Los Angeles, are based on seven years of measuring Efe children at birth and every six months thereafter. . . . The average Efe newborn was 17.6 inches long, significantly shorter than their rain forest neighbours, the Lese. By age five, an Efe child is the size of a 2½-year-old American girl.

1 Which group is being judged as normal here?
2 On what grounds are the Efe children described as falling behind on growth charts?
3 Is it likely that patterns of child development will be universal?

1.3 How do children develop?

"FIVE YEARS TO LEARN TO TALK— THAT'S NOT TOO BAD."

"WELL, I SUPPOSE I CAN LEARN TO WALK AS WELL."

"SUPPOSE I DON'T WANT TO GIVE UP NAPPIES?"

"NOBODY ASKED ME IF I WANTED A BABY BROTHER!"

Think for a moment of how much children learn and change in the years from birth to their 8th birthday. Because children are developing in this way all the time, you can easily forget the enormity of what they are managing.

If somebody wanted to set *you* such a challenging set of goals to achieve over the same number of years, you would probably think twice before agreeing! Children, of course, do not realise in babyhood what lies ahead. They take it day by day and, with the help of caring adults, achieve new skills a bit at a time. They are also very good at learning.

As you observe children, you can work out what is happening to them as they develop through the early years. Theories of child development attempt to explain, and sometimes predict, *how* this happens. They all address the central question of how much can be explained by inherited abilities and characteristics ('nature') and how much by children's experiences in childhood, including their environment ('nurture').

You might say, theory is all very interesting but what does it have to do with working with children day by day? The point is that some basic ideas from all the theories have influenced practice with children. Whether you realise it or not, already you have almost certainly been influenced by one or more of the different kinds of theories we outline in this section.

The main approaches that you are likely to come across are as follows. Please realise that these are very brief descriptions: we want to give you a flavour of the different theories. If you want to understand more, then read from the suggestions we make at the end of the section and in Appendix 3.

Biological explanations

From the 1920s onwards, Arnold Gesell and his colleagues studied many babies and children of different ages. They then described in great detail a pattern for normal development. Their explanation of development was through *maturation*. They used this word to mean patterns of change shared by all children that were triggered by the information in the genes.

Writers of advice books, such as Dr Spock, were very influenced by the maturation theory of Gesell. They included the detail of what should be happening to children at different ages. They also shared the idea that children would achieve developmental stages and skills when they were ready. This encouraged an outlook that parents should not fret and that some kinds of behaviour were phases that children would pass through without intervention.

A rather different biological explanation of human development emerged from studies of animals, for example the work of Konrad Lorenz. The suggestion here is that some patterns of human behaviour are *innate*: we are born with the tendency to behave in certain ways. This idea – that some kinds of behaviour come naturally and are not learned – has been used to explain how babies form attachments and includes the idea of bonding.

John Bowlby believed that attachment between mother and baby was a complicated set of behaviours designed to protect infants. He claimed that babies and young children would inevitably be harmed if their mother, or possibly a mother-substitute, did not care for them continuously. This belief still enters almost any discussion about child care.

Learning and development

Learning theorists play down the influence of heredity and emphasise what children *learn* from specific experiences. The focus is on behaviour – children's and adults' – and on the patterns of reward and punishment that follow what children do. Some people take an extreme behaviourist position, saying that newborn babies are born with biological reflexes but everything else is learned in response to what happens to them. This implies that all of the push for change comes from outside the individual.

John Watson applied behaviourist ideas to advice for child care. He recommended firm training of children in most areas of development and warned against adults' letting their softer feelings get in the way. For example, the idea that you can spoil babies by picking them up comes largely from Watson's approach to child care. However, it is possible to take practical ideas from learning theory and apply them with warmth.

Albert Bandura extended the basic ideas to develop social learning theory. He proposed that children could learn ways of behaving by copying what they had watched earlier. He also believed that children learned ideas and standards about behaviour which in turn influenced how they later acted. For example, Bandura believed that children's feeling of satisfaction when they achieved something could affect their behaviour.

Learning theory has been applied practically in some programmes of instruction for children, although this is probably rather more common in the United States than in Britain.

Personality and development

A number of theories explain how children develop by a combination of what *happens* to them (the outside) and what they are *feeling* (the inside). Children and adults are believed to pass through a number of stages in personal development. Their behaviour is affected by their current stage and by the lasting impact on them of earlier stages.

Psychoanalytic theories have developed from the ideas of Sigmund Freud. He believed that children's biological instincts drove their behaviour.

This led to emotional conflicts which were sometimes resolved but could cause personality problems that lasted for years.

Many writers have developed ideas in different directions from Freud's original theory. Alfred Adler, for example, was convinced that family dynamics and a child's place in the birth order of children were more important than the painful conflicts which Freud discussed. Erik Erikson, on the other hand, described a series of developmental tasks which he believed all children shared. For example, he proposed that in the first 12–18 months of life a child is struggling with a sense of basic trust, or mistrust, of those around her. He emphasised that this personal development was influenced by the society in which the child was being raised.

Development through thinking

The psychoanalytic theories emphasise children's relationships with people and feelings. Cognitive-developmental theories put more emphasis on the development of children's ability to think and make sense of the world. Consequently they also emphasise how children deal with events and objects as much as their interaction with people.

The ideas of Jean Piaget changed the direction of developmental psychology. He studied what children did when faced with different everyday situations. He then drew conclusions about how children thought about their environment at different ages. He was particularly interested in the mistakes that children made. He saw these as evidence of the differences between how *they* viewed the world and the thought processes of older children or adults. Piaget believed that children actively try to understand their environment and that this is what motivates much of their behaviour.

The cognitive-developmental theorists believe that all children pass through the same distinct stages in the same sequence. However, a given stage is not reached at the same age for everyone. Once a child has moved on to another stage, there is no going back in how she sees and makes sense of the world. For example, once a baby has realised that hidden objects are not gone forever then she searches for toys she cannot see and she plays peep-bo games. Her behaviour has changed as a result of how she now thinks about her world.

Many people have continued to test Piaget's ideas and to develop them further. Lawrence Kohlberg extended the ideas to explain how children develop a sense of right and wrong and reach moral judgments. Jerome Bruner has explored how children's developing language changes their ability to handle information.

The cognitive-developmental theories have been applied in education as well as in advice to parents. You will almost certainly have worked to help children learn through discovery for themselves. You may have discussed how to make an environment more child-centred and how to avoid making children learn facts without any meaningful context. These are practical applications of these theories.

Theory and this workbook

You will find some aspects of all the main theories in this workbook. We believe it is useful for workers to have a framework of knowledge about what kinds of development are likely to happen to children within a given age range. We do not believe that this development unfolds inevitably because of a biological programme.

There are other theories about child development. You can find out more about them in the books mentioned below. We ourselves feel more in tune with those theories that attempt to describe an interaction between children and their environment – an environment which includes the behaviour of adults. There would be no point in writing this practical workbook if we didn't believe that what you do with children and how you do it can make a vital difference.

Reading on . . .

★ Bee, Helen 1989: *The Developing Child*, 5th edn (Harper Collins).
★ Salkind, Neil J. 1985: *Theories of Human Development* (John Wiley).

1.4 Recognising children as individuals

Personal identity

Young babies behave as if there is no difference between 'me' and 'not me'. They have to learn the physical boundaries between where they end and somebody or something else begins.

By 2 years old, children see themselves partly through what they can or can't do. They are very affected by the emotional reactions of adults and other children who matter to them. They want a cuddle and a smile. They need reassurance that they are loved and in some cases that they have been forgiven for what they have just done.

Gradually, 3-, 4- and 5-year-olds develop a growing sense of self. Their feelings become part of the picture. These may be on the whole happy or sad. They also begin to see themselves in comparison with other children. They begin to relate to groups that are defined socially. A 5-year-old might be building up a sense of identity from any of the following possibilities.

Family
Do I have both parents living with me? Do I have brothers and sisters or am I an 'only'? Where do I come in the order of children – an eldest, a youngest, an in-between? What are my parents like? Do they have jobs? Does it matter if they don't? How big is my family? Are there members of the family who don't talk to each other?

Race and culture
This is linked with the family for most children. What do we believe in? Are we religious; what is our religion? What skin colour am I? Is the rest of my family the same? Are there other families around that look like us?

School and pre-school
Do I go to school or nursery? Who is in my group? Which year am I in, which class? What do the workers think of me?

Sex
Am I a boy or a girl? Should boys and girls behave differently? Is it better to be a boy or a girl?

Age
How old am I? Is it better to be older?

Friends
Who are my friends? Can I trust them, will they help me if I need them? Who are not my friends; is this a source of trouble?

I can and I can't
What can I do, what can't I do? Am I especially good at something? Does anything stop me doing things that I want?

Likes and dislikes
What do I like and dislike? Do my friends like the same things? Is it all right to disagree with my friends or my family?

Friends are part of each child's identity

ACTIVITY

1 Take the opportunity to listen in as 5- to 7-year-olds meet for the first time – perhaps in a play park. What questions do they ask? What information do they volunteer? For example, is it 'How old are you?' or 'What school do you go to?' Or do they share very little personal information?

2 Consider, on the basis of your observations, how children define themselves to their peers.

The importance of children's names

A child's name is an important, personal label. You show care and respect for children by your efforts to learn their names quickly.

Learn the name

If you have any doubts, make sure you are pronouncing the name correctly and check the spelling. You can do this without a fuss. His name may be unusual to you but it is perfectly ordinary to him. If children prefer to be known by a shortened version of their name then use that.

You shouldn't change a child's name just because you find it difficult to say. Rarely it may happen that you really cannot manage the combination of sounds that makes up a child's name. In such cases, apologise to the child and reach an agreement on how close you can get.

Use children's names

Workers with groups of children sometimes get into the bad habit of nearly always referring to the children as a group. This might be by calling out 'You lot', 'Middle room' or 'My class'.

Younger children, especially the under-3s, do not necessarily realise that you are talking to them. School-age children are more understanding about being addressed as a group. However, they appreciate and deserve the individual attention of being called by name as often as possible.

Difficulties with names

Sometimes there are problems to resolve about names. You may be unable to tell identical twins apart. Then you need to get some help from their parents in order to treat each child as an individual. Perhaps their parents can give you a hint on how to tell the two apart. Or else the children may agree to wear name badges to help you. However you manage, do avoid calling them 'the twins'.

Often there will be more than one child in a group with the same first name. Chat with children and parents to see how they would like you to resolve this. It is hard on everyone to have two children turning round every time you say 'Daniel'. The children may be happy with 'Daniel B.' and 'Daniel M.'

TO THINK ABOUT

Practical issues arise over children's names. Use some of the suggestions in the text if you are seeking to resolve them.

To help you realise that children's names matter, search your own memories of childhood. Did you experience any frustrations over your own name? For example, did adults insist on calling you by your full name when you preferred a shortened version? Did any of your friends suffer from nicknames that they disliked?

Individual patterns of behaviour

Any child is an individual in his or her own right from babyhood. You will have observed this whether you have cared for other people's children or have children of your own. You may have been surprised that even children raised in the same family can react so differently.

A part of the answer is that, strictly speaking, each child has been born into a different family. Except for twins who arrive at almost the same time, each child joins a family that is made up of different people who have had more years of experiences.

Another possible explanation is that children inherit a tendency to react in a particular way. From the early days, their reactions will be slightly different from their brothers' or sisters'. It is then very difficult, probably impossible, for parents or other carers to behave in exactly the same way to each child.

You don't have to end up in arguments over exactly how much of children's behaviour should be explained by inherited characteristics and how much is caused by how they have been treated up to now. You can take the practical approach of simply accepting that children are different and that you will have to be flexible in your behaviour.

You should treat all children fairly. You won't be able to treat them exactly the same – they won't let you do this.

Different societies tend to favour some patterns of behaviour over others. Your judgements about acceptable and good behaviour will be influenced by your own culture and upbringing.

Differences in temperament

The word 'temperament' is used in psychology to describe a pattern of reaction to other people and the environment. Writers like Alexander Thomas and Stella Chess propose that the basic pattern is inherited, but they don't claim that children are unable to change. Temperament works, if you like, as a sort of bias in the system – an individual style that you can notice in even young children.

These are a few ways of looking at how children differ in basic temperament.

How active are they?

Some children can scarcely sit still. They will need to use up some of this energy with some physical activity. Others move at a slower pace. This will be a relief to you sometimes but it can be infuriating when you want children to complete something fairly quickly, such as dressing themselves.

An ordered life or plenty of flexibility?

Some children prefer their lives to be planned out and do not like changes. They will be angry or upset if you forget to tell them about the change of plan for this afternoon. Other children enjoy change and expect you to be ready to join them at a moment's notice.

How adventurous?

Some children are ready for anything. Their sense of adventure may leave you worried for their safety. At other times you may be delighted at their willingness to perform in front of a group, when the other children are hanging back.

Some children are concerned about anything new and untried. They feel confident once they have achieved a skill. These children will need you to be patient and encouraging until they are sure of themselves.

How do they express their emotions?

All children have feelings, some just *show* them more. Some children seem to dramatise everything. If they are happy they are bubbling and enthusiastic – a joy. However, if they have a minor scratch they want quantities of bandages, and a difference of opinion with their best friend is the end of the world.

Other children keep their feelings more to themselves. You may need to deduce from small clues whether they are upset, or whether they would really like to do what you are suggesting for an activity.

How observant are they?

Some children miss nothing. Others seem to be blithely unaware of the chaos they are in or have created. The more unobservant child may need to be told rather carefully how to do things since she may not have really watched you. The observant child will want to know why you are doing it differently now, or changing what you said last time.

Are they easily distracted?

Some children flit like butterflies from one thing to another. They go with what attracts their attention. They may pick up a lot of interest and information on the way. However, you may worry that they do not concentrate long enough to see one thing through to completion.

Other children show great persistence. When they set their mind on achieving something, they are determined to see it through. This persistence may irritate you if you want to change the direction of a group.

TO THINK ABOUT

Some of the children in your care will be more similar to you in temperament than others.

1 Give some thought to the concept of match and mismatch between temperaments if you are experiencing a difficult relationship with a child.

For example, *you* might be naturally very outgoing and find it surprising that one child is so reserved and needs so much encouragement to join in.

2 Look at the setting in which you work. In your opinion, is it is organised in such a way that, say, children need great persistence to enjoy the activities available?

Helping children stretch

Whatever the reason, some of these differences persist through life into adulthood. Children can learn to stretch themselves, adapt and experiment. You can help them in this.

Observe how children tend to react to situations. Accept children as they are – with their strong points and vulnerabilities. Help them to be more flexible in their behaviour.

Perhaps Toby will always be slightly more cautious than Asif. Bahaar may always be a bit more confident in trying new things than Sandra. This doesn't matter, so long as none of the children feel that they are absolutely stuck as they are. Nor should they be made to feel that there is something the matter with them because their approach is different from that of another child.

Reading on . . .

★ If you want to read more about temperament, you could start with the discussion in Helen Bee's *The Developing Child*, 5th edn (Harper Collins, 1989). She gives other references that you can follow up for more detail.

Happy children?

Children need to feel happy with themselves as individuals. They need to feel confident that they are worth something. Poor food can stunt children's physical growth. There is also the question of *emotional* growth, and children who have a very low opinion of themselves are unlikely to make the best of their abilities. Children who actually dislike themselves will find it hard even to accept compliments from you.

You will see through children's behaviour whether they have a positive view of themselves. They will be ready to try something new. They will not be seriously upset by what other children say. A child who doubts herself will be less willing to try, more easily disheartened, and more likely to tell you 'I'm no good'.

Children will not be smiling all the time; that would not be a realistic hope. Your aim is to help them to feel happy about how they are and optimistic about what they can do. You can help them in the following ways.

Create an encouraging environment
You have some control over the environment in which you care for children and greet their families. It matters how *you* behave day by day: your behaviour gives a message to the children as loud as your words. You are also offering a model for children to imitate in how they behave to one another.

Deal firmly and positively with threats to children's sense of self-worth
You will need to be ready to look at your own assumptions and prejudices as well as to deal with the impact of the prejudices of others. Look in Chapter 7 for more on this.

Help children to deal with disabilities or health problems
These make a very real difference to their childhood: how can you help them to be positive? Section 3.4 has ideas about this.

Treat children as individuals, separate from their behaviour
Children need to feel confident that you like them. You will be cross
sometimes about what they have *done*, but this should not threaten your
feelings *about them as people*. This is a crucial part of how you behave with
children. We return to what it means in Chapter 7.

2 Good practice with the under-8s

2.1 Principles and good practice

Who says what is good practice?

The considered view of what makes good practice comes from:

- people who work directly with young children, and those who advise them;
- the practical application of research about young children and their families;
- what the law lays down that you must or must not do.

In this section we sum up some general principles for you, and give briefly some information about what research and the law contribute to the overall picture of good practice.

An outlook to support good practice

If you are going to work well with children and their families, you need to develop a particular outlook. We have summed this up in the following points.

Your work is important

Working with the under-8s is a most valuable job. You may need to remind yourself of this since the work is often undervalued.

Parenting is an equally important task. The key point about partnership with parents (section 2.4) is that you aim to work *together*, not to be in competition or argument over the children.

Working for good practice is continuous

Good practice never stops. It is not something that you achieve and then sit back to enjoy. Even very experienced workers should be willing to take a new look at what they have been doing and to develop their practice.

Opinions change over the years. For example, current views on what should be done in partnership with parents or on equal opportunities are different from ten years ago. So part of good practice has to be the

Children enjoy making things

willingness to reassess what you are doing, as an individual worker or as a whole centre or group.

Good practice includes thinking as well as doing

Caring workers are ready to think about what they do as well as to get on and do it. Sometimes you need to ask yourself questions about how you are working and your reasons for doing it that way.

Consider your assumptions

Everyone is raised and lives within a particular culture. You too will have made assumptions about child care and family life: this is inevitable. Good practice requires you to listen and try to understand the assumptions of people raised differently from you. Be ready to question your own assumptions and to revise how you behave in the light of what you learn.

You are an individual

Chapter 1 of this workbook stresses that each child is an individual. So, of course, are you. Good practice does *not* mean that all workers behave in exactly the same way or say the same things.

Children and parents want an individual approach. Your work should be guided by a framework for good practice that you share with other workers. However, this can be achieved with a personal style and your own individuality.

Important principles underlying practice

Good practice shows through your behaviour day by day. The following basic principles of practice should be communicated by what you do. Similar principles underlie the NVQs/SVQs and the guidelines that we have listed at the end of the section.

Showing that you care
Children should feel confident that you really care about what happens to them. At the most basic, they should believe that you are pleased to see them and that you notice when they are absent.

You show your caring attitude towards parents through respect for their views and their experience. Your behaviour needs to show that you want to work with them rather than take over.

Seeing children as whole individuals
You need a good knowledge of children under 8 in general, but you have to use this recognising that each child is an individual. Children share interests and ways of looking at the world, yet each boy and girl is unique. You need to look for and respect whatever makes each child individual.

Look through the children's eyes
You need to be ready to listen to children and to watch them. If you do this, you will be more able to see their points of view and to judge whether their needs are being met. You can also enjoy the rather different way in which young children look at the world.

Children need to be involved in doing

Young children learn most easily when they are active. They need to be exploring and trying things out. Of course, the under-8s can learn by watching and listening but they find it hard to be a quiet audience for very long.

Partnership with parents

Parents will continue to be responsible for their children long after the children have moved on from your care. Undoubtedly you will hope that parents will respect your skills and experience. In your turn, you should respect parents' relationship with their own children and the unique knowledge that this gives. Section 2.4 discusses partnership in more detail.

Co-operation with other workers

You need to work together with other adults who are involved with the same children or families. Children deserve a consistent approach from workers who are jointly responsible for a group.

Equal opportunities

This principle, like all the others, runs throughout your practice, regardless of the exact mix of children and families with whom you work. We discuss in section 2.3 what 'equal opportunities' means.

Reading on . . .

The following guides are very practical (you will find the addresses in Appendix 2).
★   Cowley, Liz 1991: *Young Children in Group Day Care – guidelines for good practice* (National Children's Bureau).
★   Kids Club Network 1989: *Guidelines of Good Practice for Out-of-School Care Schemes.*
★   National Childminding Association 1992: *Setting the Standards.*
★   Pre-school Playgroups Association: *Guidelines.* The PPA has published a number of booklets covering guidelines for full-day and sessional care.

ACTIVITY

Think about the following and make yourself some notes about your experience and knowledge. Be positive about what you have to offer to children and their parents.

You can use this activity to gather your own thoughts privately. If the activity is done in a group, then the group leader should establish rules of confidentiality and people's right to decline to share the more personal experiences.

1   I have spent time with babies and children aged. . . .
2   I have spent time with children in the following different settings. . . .
3   I enjoy the following activities that I can share with children. . . .
4   I am particularly good at the following activities which I can share with children. . . .
5   I have had these experiences in my life that I believe give me insight into how children or parents may feel. . . .
6   I have relevant, helpful knowledge in these areas. . . .

*You bring your own skills to your work
in helping children*

ACTIVITY

1 Try to remember what was normal behaviour in your own family during your childhood. You could make brief notes on any of the following:

- behaviour at mealtimes (for example, table manners);
- what your family ate or did not eat;
- how children were expected to speak to adults;
- who did the household tasks (only adults? only daughters?);
- the kind of behaviour that got you into most trouble;
- family phrases that still go through your mind (for example, 'Courtesy costs nothing').

2 Look over your notes and consider the possible sources of your family's ways. What do you think was the impact of how your parents themselves had been raised? (They may, of course, have deliberately done the opposite to your grandparents.) Looking back, can you see the influence of your family's culture or religious beliefs?

3 Perhaps you were not raised within a family home. If you spent your childhood in a residential children's home, how do you think you have built up a picture of what a family is and how one works?

2.2 Good practice and the law

Some aspects to good practice are determined by law. For example, nobody has been permitted to use physical discipline on children in English, Welsh or Scottish state schools since this was made illegal in the 1986 Education Act.

Some brief information follows about the 1976 Race Relations Act and the 1989 Children Act. There are, of course, other pieces of legislation relevant to good practice. If you want more information, start with the Department of Health's volumes of guidance to the Children Act.

The Children Act 1989

The Act and all the associated Regulations are very detailed. They deal with private disputes between parents about children, court orders and care proceedings as well as with day care and fostering. Primary aims are to protect children, to prevent family breakdown, and to ensure minimum standards in services for children and their families. Many such services have to be registered and inspected by the local authority, including day care and childminding of the under-8s. The local authority is responsible for ensuring that acceptable standards are met.

The key principles emphasised throughout the Act are these:

- *The primary concern* The welfare of children must be the *prime* concern of workers and authorities.
- *The role of parents*   Parents have responsibilities towards their children – they do not have absolute rights as if children were possessions.
- *Sharing care*   Workers and authorities should work in partnership with parents.
- *Children's individuality*   In the provision of services local authorities must take into account each child's and each family's racial origin, religious persuasion, and cultural and linguistic background.
- *Disabilities*   Children with disabilities are specifically included with 'children in need' as defined in the Act.

Reading on . . .

The National Children's Bureau highlights on the Act will give you a good framework for making sense of it. These are:

- ★   No. 91, *Overview of the Children Act 1989*, by Peter Smith;
- ★   No. 100, *The Children Act 1989 and Day Care*, by Peter Elfer;
- ★   No. 109, *The Children Act 1989 and Disability*, by Philippa Russell.

Several volumes of Department of Health guidance support the legislation. Most useful to you would be:

- ★   Volume 2, *Family Support, Day Care and Educational Provision*;
- ★   Volume 6, *Children with Disabilities*.

If you are working in a centre or similar place for children which has to be registered under the Children Act, you may want to know more about what the Act means for you. Your local authority should have produced material to explain the requirements of the Act and the minimum standards that they require.

The Race Relations Act 1976

This Act made it unlawful to discriminate on racial grounds in four ways:

- *through direct discrimination* – for example, refusing a child admission to a day nursery, because he or she is black;
- *through indirect discrimination* – for example, applying a condition which in practice favours one group over another (if this requirement cannot be justified on *non*-racial grounds then it is unlawful discrimination);
- *by segregation* – for example, having all black children sit together at a table for the sole reason that they are black;
- *by victimisation* – for example, if a child were excluded from a nursery because his or her parents had complained previously about discrimination in the nursery.

All of the above apply to all racial groups. The Act does not enable people to insist that someone has broken the law without offering proof: there must be careful consideration of what has happened in order to decide whether someone has indeed acted against the law.

For further information

Try these organisations:
★ Children's Legal Centre, 20 Compton Terrace, London N1 2UN (*tel.* 071–359 6251).
★ Commission for Racial Equality: Elliot House, 10–12 Allington Street, London SW1E 5EH (*tel.* 071–828 7022).
★ Early Years Trainers Anti-Racist Network (EYTARN): The Lyndens, 51 Granville Road, London N12 0JH (*tel.* 081–446 7056).

2.3 Equal opportunities

The principle of equal opportunities is summarised well by the following statement:

> Through the ways in which they work, staff should demonstrate that they positively value and respect children of all ethnic origins/racial groups, religions, cultures, linguistic backgrounds, and abilities. Children of both sexes should be positively encouraged by staff to participate in **all** activities.
>
> Liz Cowley 1991: *Young Children in Group Day Care*, p. 44
> (National Children's Bureau). [Emboldening in original.]

Equal opportunities is significant for your work, regardless of the exact mix of children in your care. This is because your responsibility is twofold: you have a responsibility to individual children and their source of personal identity; you can also contribute to what any child is learning about other people and the world.

Your response to individual children

Your job is to help individual children to feel positively about themselves. You cannot do this unless you recognise that children's race, their sex, and their level of ability and any disabilities are *all* part of them – their identity.

You cannot promote equal opportunities by saying, 'I treat children all the same.' This does not work, because children are not the same. You need to show through your behaviour and your use of resources that you positively recognise and respect the differences between individual children.

Of course, you should treat all children fairly. However, you are not behaving in a fair way if some of the children with whom you work rarely see people like themselves in the stories on the bookshelf or if hurtful remarks from other children go unchallenged.

What you offer to all children

All children deserve a range of experiences and an environment that encourage a positive outlook towards people whom they may see as different from themselves.

For example, the series of publications that we recommend in Chapters 3, 5 and 6 are of two sorts. On the one hand, some are informative about different parts of the world and different cultures, while others inform about health problems that children, and adults, may not fully understand. On the other, we recommend many of the books and series simply because they depict children from different racial groups, children of both sexes and sometimes children with obvious disabilities just getting on with their lives. They are in the books as children.

Children can and do learn prejudiced attitudes from their early years. These attitudes affect their behaviour towards other people, whom they view as different from them or 'not normal'. Prejudices do real harm to the children who are on the receiving end of such abuse or dismissive comments. In section 1.4 we stress that children need and deserve to feel happy with themselves as individuals. Children who express the prejudices may feel superior: it is not morally right that anybody should boost their own confidence by putting others down.

It's good to see men with babies

What can you do?

Your most positive approach is to view the principle of equal opportunities as running throughout your work. You will find suggestions for making this happen in every part of this workbook. The only reason that we have written this separate section on equal opportunities is to explain exactly what we mean by the words.

You can work positively for equal opportunities in the following ways.

Be ready to examine your own attitudes

Good practice depends on being prepared to look closely at your own assumptions and beliefs. Be ready to revise these if necessary. For example, section 3.2 may help you reconsider beliefs about a normal diet that you have never got round to questioning.

Gather more knowledge

You can continue to learn new information and to test out the accuracy of what you have already learned. You can extend your knowledge by talking with people, by reading and by watching relevant television programmes.

We give suggestions for reading material in every part of this workbook. You will find that some of the series we recommend for children will be equally informative for you.

Take any opportunities offered to chat with people whose life experience is different from your own. This will not always be possible, and of course we are not suggesting that you should pry. A good alternative is to read personal accounts of how it feels to be treated as different. Some of the fiction for teenage readers is excellent: for example, if you need an insight into what it is like to be black in a largely white society try *Sumitra's Story* by Rukshana Smith (Bodley Head), or *My Mate Shofiq* by Jan Needle (Penguin Lions).

Extend your skills

Several sections of the workbook will specifically help here. Chapter 5, for instance, has ideas about communication. You need to be ready to support children who feel bad about themselves as a result of the prejudices of others. This means being ready to deal with rude remarks to children that attack their self-esteem. Section 7.3 has a suggested pattern of action.

TO THINK ABOUT

1 Be prepared to ask yourself:

- 'What am I assuming?'
- 'What's my reason for this assumption?'
- 'Does my reason stand up to challenge?'

A few examples may help you to develop an awareness of unchecked assumptions.

(a) Assumptions about normal child development are often grounded in one particular culture. It is not sensible to assess a child's physical coordination by whether she can use a knife and fork unless this is the normal way of eating meals in her family.

(b) Perhaps you feel comfortable making a generalisation like 'Boys aren't interested in babies.' Try replacing 'boys' with 'tall children'. Does this phrase seem silly? What makes it acceptable to generalise about a large group such as all boys or all girls?

(c) People with little experience of disability can be very rude to disabled fellow-adults. One assumption seems to be that sitting in a wheelchair is evidence that a person is unable to talk or to understand normal conversation.

2 If you accept the need to question your own assumptions, then you may be more able to challenge other people's. It is important that you do this in a way that helps them rethink and not feel under attack. It is a case of saying something like 'Have you looked at it this way?' rather than 'That's a stupid thing to say.'

CASE STUDY

Whiteoak playgroup is in a small town surrounded by rolling countryside. The local population is entirely white.

The county Under-8s Advisor has run two workshops with the playgroup staff to explore the principles of equal opportunities. These were motivated by the requirements of the Children Act 1989.

In the first workshop the staff could not see the point. They argued, 'We have no black children here, so what has all this got to do with us?' However, they agreed to do some observations and a bit of thinking before they met again.

In the second workshop, three main points emerged through the discussion:

(a) Some children have already learned a very stereotyped view of black people. One worker reports a conversation with two 4-year-olds who refused to believe that a male teacher could ever be black, because 'black people do boxing'. Another child talked sadly about black children as if they were always ill and starving: this is the image she sees in posters on the wall of the church hall.

(b) In the first workshop, staff were adamant that they should not be trying to influence children's attitudes. Since then it has struck one worker that they *do* set out to do this, it is just that they are not keen to tackle children's *race* attitudes. She reminds the group that they had the theme of consideration for other people's feelings. So the staff do believe that under-5s are developing attitudes and ways of behaving towards others.

(c) The playgroup staff pride themselves on widening the children's horizons beyond their own backyards. They discuss the recent project with the children on flight and planes. Very few of the children have so far travelled on a plane and staff wanted them to think beyond their own experience.

1   Do you work in an all-white area? Are you assuming that equal opportunities on race is just for areas with a racial mix?

2   Have you heard any of the children in your care expressing stereotyped views of races other than their own?

3   What could be the first changes for Whiteoak playgroup to consider?

2.4 Partnership with parents

Partnership will have a different meaning in practice depending on where you are working. However, the basics will always be the same:

- Make friendly contact with the parents of children for whom you are responsible.
- Behave towards parents with courtesy and a respect for how important they are to their children.
- Offer ways to build continuity between parents' care of their child and your own work.

A working relationship

Friendly but not friends

A friendly face is always welcome

Mostly you will make contact with parents because you are caring for their children. A good relationship will be friendly, but you are *not* making friends: the ground rules are different. If the child of one of your friends attends your place of work, you will both have to sort out the two different kinds of relationship.

Openness and honesty

You should be honest and open with parents about those aspects of your work that affect their child. In your first meetings you should explain to parents the normal pattern of the day that you are offering children.

You should ask their permission before making changes in the usual day such as taking children out for trips. You should not allow people access to the children without asking permission of the parents. This is true even with fully accredited professionals such as doctors or researchers.

Confidentiality

All parents must be able to feel confident that their lives will not be fuel for gossip. This includes conversations between you and other staff as well as those with parents. However, you need to be honest in your first contacts with parents about the circumstances under which you could *not* promise to keep a secret: events that could affect a child's well-being or safety would have to be passed on to colleagues or your senior.

Contracts or other agreements

Some centres for children and their families now use a written agreement or contract. This might detail the hours of the service you offer, any payment involved, and what happens if parents do not bring a child regularly.

Sometimes a contract also includes details of the work that a centre is planning to undertake with a child or family. It is then sensible for workers and parents to meet formally every 3–6 months to review the arrangements and check whether any changes are appropriate.

A contract can help by drawing up the boundaries to the relationship between parents and a centre or school. It is one way of saying what you expect from parents and what they can confidently expect from you. No contract will cover everything that might arise – it would get far too long.

A contract will not help much:

- if the obligations are all one-way, for example if parents have a long list to which *they* have to agree but *you* are not committing yourself to much at all;
- if nothing happens if parents break their side of the agreement, for example if they regularly bring their children in late.

Additionally in the latter case, the parents who do hold to the rules will become very irritated.

Communication and courtesy

What matters above all is how you *behave* towards parents. You may *feel* friendly but if this rarely shows through your smiles or when you are chatting with parents, they will never realise.

Be ready to make the first move. For example, if you work in a playgroup or a school, recognise that some parents may see this as your territory and feel ill at ease.

If your work extends into helping parents with problems, you will need to learn counselling skills – this is a specialist area which we are not trying to cover here. Don't underestimate the importance of everyday courtesy and short conversations with parents.

Remember some of the basic rules that make others feel comfortable and respected. Much of this is equally important in your communication with children. In brief everyday contact:

- *Acknowledge that a parent is present*   If words aren't easy, then smile or nod. When possible, acknowledge that a parent is leaving by a wave or by saying goodbye. (Obviously a personal approach is less possible if you have a number of parents arriving and leaving together.)
- *Use parents' names in the way that they wish*   Not everyone wants to be called by their first name. Parents don't usually mind being called 'Maria's Mum' or 'Owen's Dad', so long as that is not the *only* way they are addressed. Note that not all cultures share the Western order of personal name followed by family name. If in doubt, ask what you should call a parent and how you should pronounce a name.

When you are talking or if a parent clearly wants to talk with you:

- *Apologise* if you have to keep someone waiting.
- *Give your full attention* to what is being said. If you have to break off, perhaps to deal with a child, apologise for the interruption.
- *Show that you are listening* by looking at the other person from time to time. Be alert to whether the other person is comfortable with a direct gaze.
- *Be alert* to the other person's comfortable speaking distance from you. If someone backs away, you are probably too close.
- *Make brief comments of your own* to show that you are listening and interested.
- *Check that you have understood each other* if that seems necessary. It helps if you summarise briefly what needs to be done or the nature of the problem.

- *Remove barriers* to easy communication. For example, if the other person is considerably shorter than you or in a wheelchair find a place to sit down.

Using words

You will not always share a language with parents. If you work in a multilingual area, it is important that any written material from your workplace is available in the languages spoken locally. You need also to find someone who could be called on to help you communicate with a parent who speaks a language that you do not.

People who speak the same language do not always use the same words. Most workers who share skills have some words and phrases which are not in everyday use outside the job. The following suggestions could help you be aware of the words that you use:

- Ask friends who are not in your line of work to stop you when what you say about work doesn't make sense to them.
- Avoid using the shorthand of initial letters. If you work in a school you will know what 'SATs' means, but parents may not.
- Look at the words you use on displays about projects or programmes with the children. Are these described in a more complicated way than necessary? Parents do not usually chat about their children's motor skills or their social-emotional development. There are simpler ways of putting the point, and without being patronising.
- If you really need to use technical terms then be ready to explain them.

'Parents' means dads as well!

Difficult conversations

Neither you nor a child's parent will feel satisfied with a conversation which is largely one-way. You will want parents to listen to you and to consider what you have to say. They will want, and deserve, the same respect.

You will set the scene for a more useful exchange by your behaviour. You may find these suggestions particularly useful if you are communicating problems or concerns about a child; however, they are equally useful in conversations which you don't approach with trepidation.

Don't present your opinions as facts

You can be honest about your opinions about a child and her behaviour. However, these are just your opinions.

Two things are equally important here:

- Choose your words to show that you are not loading all your frustrations onto the child or her parents.
- Give parents the chance to express *their* opinions – which may be different.

For example, you may have genuine difficulties with 4-year-old Janie. However, if you say to her parents something like 'Your daughter has an awful temper', you are putting all the problems onto Janie. Her parents may well defend their daughter and then an argument can begin.

The message comes over differently, however, if you explain how you are feeling: 'I find it hard work handling Janie's temper tantrums.' With this phrase you are communicating that you feel there is a problem, but you are creating an opportunity to discuss with the parents what is happening and what might be done.

Focus on children's behaviour

Focus on what children do, and not on guesses as to why or giving them personality labels. Avoid describing a child through her behaviour. (Chapter 7 returns to this topic.)

For example, you might talk with a parent about your concerns that Kevin hits other children on a regular basis. Explore what you could both do about this. Don't start with the claim that Kevin is 'an aggressive boy': this implies that he cannot change, and is likely to put his parent on the defensive.

Good news too

Even when you are at your wits' end with a child and her behaviour, do your utmost to find something positive to say to her parent. You owe this to the child as well (Chapter 7 again).

Listen

Give parents a chance to talk early on in the conversation. Don't insist on delivering everything you want to say before you are ready to listen.

If parents are expressing doubts about you or the setting in which you work, then listen. Don't leap to your own defence or get irritated: allow that parents may have a point. Make sure that you understand what is being said to you. Explain briefly, if you feel this is necessary. In other words, give them the respect that you would like to receive.

Communicating your values

Partnership with parents means an exchange of expertise, ideas and opinions. Ideally, if you chat with parents they will come to understand more about how you work and you will come to understand their way of raising their children. Part of good practice for you is also to extend your understanding of cultural and religious differences as one way in which parents may approach children and child care differently from you. (See section 2.3, which explains equal opportunities.)

However, you will not agree with all parents on all matters. You owe it to them:

- to explain in straightforward terms the key values that underpin how you work with the children;
- to be honest about how this means that you behave with children, and what you are, and are not, willing to do.

For example, some parents may disagree with you on your refusal to use smacking as a form of discipline. The principle of partnership with parents does not mean that you have to implement all wishes expressed by parents: it does mean, though, that you owe them an honest explanation when you are not willing or are genuinely unable to follow their wishes. Different parts of the workbook will help you with reasons for your practice.

Play + learning

Let parents know that children will get messy

Practical ways of involving parents

Settling children

Children vary a great deal in how long they take to settle themselves with a new carer and a new situation. Some practical steps can ease the process for the child, the parent and yourself. You need to be clear about how you would like the settling-in period to work and how you decide that a child looks settled.

- *Invite parents to stay* with their child – don't be rigid about how long they must stay.
- *Be ready to make parents welcome* and offer suggestions about what they could do in the group.
- *Be ready to help them to separate* from their child in stages.

If you do not have children of your own, understand that the settling process is difficult for parents as well as children. Parents are people too, with feelings. Ideally, parents would like a delicate balance of emotions from their child – a bit of sadness so that the parent does not feel unwanted but not so much distress that the parent feels terrible at leaving the child.

When children move on

You can work together with parents to ease the process when children move on – within one setting or to a new one (for instance, to school from a playgroup). Such changes can be stressful for children, especially if they are leaving most or all of their playmates behind.

You can work in co-operation with parents:

- to warn a child that a change is coming, and when;
- to talk about what will be happening, answer a child's questions, and deal with any worries;
- to encourage children to think positively about the next stage, as part of growing up;
- to visit the next setting, even if it is just a different room in the same building;
- to help a child to learn, or to gain more confidence in skills that will ease his entry into the next setting.

Invitations to meetings

Parents will sometimes ask to speak with you. If they feel comfortable with you, then this will seem very natural. You may organise an opportunity for parents to visit the group or to see children's work. Either kind of meeting will go better when you have a friendly everyday relationship with parents. They will feel more able to contribute if you have kept them well informed on how their child is settling into the group and what she enjoys doing.

You may plan a meeting of general interest, perhaps with an invited speaker. Parents who do not want or are unable to come to such meetings will still wish to be kept informed about their child. Parents have the right to be consulted about programmes or any treatment for their child and to be asked their opinion about more general aspects to nursery, centre or hospital life.

You may be involved in an individual and more formal meeting with

parents. For example, some day nurseries and family centres hold regular reviews. It is possible to make any meeting more comfortable for parents.

- *Chat with parents before the meeting*   They need to know what to expect, for example how the meeting will be run and who will be there.
- *Be ready to consider how a parent might feel*   For instance, how would *you* feel if you walked into a room full of strangers and you were not introduced?
- *Be considerate in taking notes*   It is sometimes necessary to make notes in a meeting: this can be done in a friendly and respectful way. Explain to parents the reason for making notes and give them a copy.
- *Seat parents so that they feel part of the meeting*   It can be very daunting to face a number of people, especially if they are, for example, behind a large table.
- *Would the parents like company?*   Parents may like to be accompanied and to sit next to a worker whom they know well.

EXAMPLES

(a) Michael

Michael lives very close to the nursery where he works. Within the last week one parent has started to knock on his door, bringing her child with her and expecting Michael to take her daughter to the nursery with him when he goes to work.

1   Do you think it is apropriate for Michael to be asked to do this?
2   What if other parents start to do the same thing?
3   How should Michael handle this?

(b) Simone

Simone works in a unit for children with serious disabili-ties. She knows that many of the parents have problems in getting babysitters. Two of her colleagues have sat for families in the evening. Simone does not want to do this but feels bad about saying 'No'.

1   Do you think it is acceptable for Simone to refuse requests to sit in the evening?
2   Does her unit need a policy on where work begins and ends?

Comment

A friendly relationship with parents does not mean that you have to agree to anything that is asked of you. If you are doubtful about something, you may want to talk it over with colleagues or ask a more senior worker for guidance.

TO THINK ABOUT

You are offering a service to parents. You can try to look at your practice from another angle, by remembering times that you have been on the receiving end of a service.

1   How does it feel when you are treated with courtesy at the dentist or in high-street shops? Or when people greet you pleasantly or apologise if something has gone wrong?
2   How do you feel when you are treated dismissively or made to wait for ages?
3   What experiences have you had when you wished to make a complaint?
4   What lessons can you draw for your own work?

CASE STUDIES

There can be many different patterns in offering involvement to parents. A programme of activities that would work well in one setting for children and their parents might be inappropriate or unrealistic in another.

The two descriptions that follow are examples of involving parents in very different settings.

1 York Children's Centre

Parents are always invited to join centre trips and usually at least half-a-dozen parents do join in. The head of the centre has learned to make it very clear that any adult coming on a trip has responsibility for a number of children and does not simply disappear at the destination.

A spare room has been made into a parents' room and equipped with tea and coffee; currently there is a heated argument between the smoking and the non-smoking parents about the rule for the room. One member of staff arranges meetings with speakers on topics that parents request: these meetings are usually very well attended.

A regular parents' group stopped a year ago when the head of centre became concerned that, although very successful as a support group for those attending, the group had closed itself to any new arrivals.

2 Greenbridge Primary School

This school has a flourishing association of 'Friends of Greenbridge', which has regular meetings and organises fetes and jumble sales.

Parents are made welcome if they offer to help out within the school. The head prefers that parents do not work with their own child's class and that teachers know in advance when a parent will be helping.

The school has offered a number of information evenings as well as termly open evenings for individual discussions about children. One or two general meetings have developed into arguments between some parents and teachers about reading methods and standards.

1　The centre and the school are different settings, established for different purposes. Think about the setting in which you work. What kinds of parent involvement are under consideration?
2　Both York and Greenbridge have faced the dilemma on some practical issues of whose decision counts. How does your setting resolve disagreements or different perspectives between staff and parents?
3　Take the opportunity to discuss involving parents with colleagues or friends who have experience of different settings.

Reading on . . .

★　Pugh, Gillian and Erica De'Ath 1989: *Working towards partnership in the early years* (National Children's Bureau).
★　Laishley, Jennie 1987: *Working with Young Children*, Part Four (Hodder & Stoughton).

And specifically for working with parents of children with disabilities:

★　McConkey, Roy 1985: *Working with Parents: a practical guide for teachers and therapists* (Croom Helm).
★　Shah, Robina 1992: *The Silent Minority – children with disabilities in Asian families* (National Children's Bureau).

2.5 Organising children's environment

There will be many aspects of your working environment that you cannot change. The same will be true of the larger environment in which your workplace is situated. Our aim in this section and in section 2.6 is to help you think afresh about your immediate environment with the children and to make the most of what you have.

First impressions

You know how to navigate your way around the building in which you work and how to find your room. Can you remember your first day and the experience of finding your way around?

TO THINK ABOUT

Imagine yourself as a parent, visiting for the first time. If this is difficult, then ask parents about *their* experiences.

1 Is it easy to get lost?
2 Is it easy to find the main office?
3 How long is it before a worker is likely to notice and greet a parent or any other visitor?
4 Are there helpful notices? Do these assume that people can read and that they speak one particular language?
5 How easily could anyone move around the building pushing a double buggy? In a wheelchair?

Child's-eye view

Some nurseries and centres have facilities such as toilets or tables adjusted to children's size. Most homes are built to suit adults who are taller than most children. You may need to make adjustments to help children.

The world looks different from toddler height

ACTIVITY

Sit down, or bend at the knees, and spend some time with your eyes at the height of a child's eyes.

1   Look around you. What can you see?
2   Are the decorations at the right height for children?
3   Are there corners of furniture at head-banging height?
4   Do the adults spend a lot of time standing up, such that they usually look down to children?

5   Could children get to toys or choose books without help? Equally – can they reach coffee cups or other things that should be safely out of their reach?
6   How might children experience this environment if they had problems of mobility, limited vision or hearing?

Children often enjoy small spaces

Using space

You are working in a particular room or set of rooms. There will be some things you can change but some things you will just have to live with. It will help if you take a fresh look at the physical space where you spend time with children.

How big is the room in which you work? If it is rather small, you will need to plan some activities that get you and the children out of the room for a change of scene and a chance to spread yourselves. If you work in a nursery or playgroup, can you use any shared space or corridors? Can you spread into the garden in good weather?

If you work in a large room the noise and bustle may get overwhelming. Do the children tend to dash about? Can you rearrange chairs or bookcases to create quiet corners? If there are several workers in one large room, can you organise your day so that the adults stay with an activity, encouraging children to stay put?

Keeping children safe

Children need both to be safe and to feel safe. In reality, it is impossible to design for children an environment in which they could never hurt themselves; and if you did manage to do so, it would almost certainly be very boring. Your job is to reduce the risks to an acceptable level.

However careful you are, sometimes she will fall

• You need to keep alert all the time to what children are doing.
• You need to try to teach about potential dangers without nagging.

Babies and younger children need a high level of supervision: they have a very limited understanding of actual danger, and they don't grasp why you are worried about them. Section 3.3 has suggestions about teaching children to keep themselves safe.

First aid and accidents

You need to have a first aid box, and everyone should know where it is stored. In a centre at least one person should be recently qualified in first aid.

If you work in a nursery or centre, there should be a record book for accidents. Anything more than a very minor bump should be written down. If a child has been accidentally hurt during the day or session, who is responsible for telling the parent? You should be clear about this: a parent will be understandably annoyed and concerned if he or she discovers a large bruise or graze and nobody has said anything.

Emergencies

You should have a plan of how to get yourself and the children out of the building in the event of an emergency such as fire. There should be at least two possible routes. If you are working with other people, you should all know the emergency drill and practise this regularly.

Strangers and visitors

Some settings for children are more vulnerable than others to the arrival of strangers who have no business there. You may have to make decisions that balance security against the desire to welcome people who do have good reason to be there.

However, it is disruptive for the children if you have many visitors, especially if there is little or no warning that they are coming. You should be told in advance of any visitors to your workplace; you can then tell the children who is coming and why he or she is visiting. Obviously, exactly what you say will depend on the age of the children and the stage of their language development.

Children will come to recognise a regular visitor such as the doctor. If you have students on placement, you can explain how they will be working with the group.

Prior warning of visitors is respectful to you and to the children. It is also safer for children: you don't want them to feel that it's acceptable for people whom they do not know to start talking or playing with them.

Can the children wander off?

You should be organised to ensure that children cannot wander off without anybody realising. Check that gates are shut and that children cannot climb over or through surrounding fences. If you work in a large group, each worker should have a primary responsibility for a small number of children: you are then more likely to notice quickly if someone is missing.

CASE STUDY

Beckmead School has two entrances. This is convenient for staff and families as they can enter from either of two roads. However, other people use the school playground as a cut through, despite notices requesting them not to do so. A few have used the playground toilets as if these were public conveniences.

Two incidents bring matters to a head. A member of staff politely questions a woman crossing the playground in the morning break. The woman becomes very abusive and threatens the worker. A few days later, two children are frightened by a man who claims he is looking for the office and then starts a sexually suggestive conversation with them.

The head discusses the problem at an emergency staff meeting. It is decided that one entrance will remain locked except for fifteen minutes either side of the start and end times for school, including nursery hours. A letter goes out to parents to explain what is happening and the reason.

1   Is your workplace vulnerable to strangers wandering in without reason?
2   How can you make the setting safe and yet still be welcoming to people who have good reason to be there?

Ratio of adults to children

In *The Children Act: Guidance and Regulations, Volume 2: Family Support, Day Care and Educational Provision for Young Children* (HMSO, 1991), the Department of Health recommends minimum ratios in day care, playgroups and educational services:

- 1 adult to every 3 children of 0–2 years;
- 1 adult to every 4 children of 2–3 years;
- 1 adult to every 8 children of 3–7 years.

These numbers are the *minimum* ratios of adults to children – you would expect to have fewer children per adult if some of those children had special needs.

Children need to get out and about and they enjoy even local outings to the shops or the market: the ratios given above would not be safe for such trips. Children, especially those under 3 or even 4 years, may dash off without warning and at high speed. The *most* you should attempt is one younger child secure in a buggy and an older child on each side of you, holding onto your hand or the buggy handle.

You can trust school-age children rather more to stay by you but they still tend to wander. You should not be responsible for more children than you can easily keep in sight – really no more than four.

Outings that involve a lot of physical activity need even more careful supervision and so fewer children per adult. For example, swimming trips should not be attempted unless you have one adult per child under 5: these adults should be in the water with the children. If the children are older and can swim, check on the recommended ratio with your local pool: however, you cannot keep a watchful eye on more than five or six swimming children.

Involving children

You are responsible for the organisation of the children's environment, but you can involve the children themselves in many ways.

Children feel involved if they can make some decisions. They like sometimes to choose the book for story time or to select the pictures for a display. Give children an opportunity to express their opinion on a recent trip or a new recipe for cakes.

Even young children should have a role in maintaining their environment; you should not end up with all the tidying and sorting. Although some children may need firm encouragement, many are flattered to be trusted with a task.

Organise your day so that there is time for children to help you. You need to make the tidying up seem an attractive activity and a natural part of the day. Children will be discouraged if there is too much rush. With your guidance, young children are quite good at tidying up. Keep them company and don't expect them to be perfect. Organise one or two searchers when necessary to track down lost pieces of jigsaw or missing toys.

You can make an enjoyable activity out of organising a cupboard or a shelf. On a hot day, equip the children with aprons and set about a special scrub-up of plastic toys or the chairs.

TO THINK ABOUT

1   Is your setting well organised to encourage children to get involved? Are there changes that would help? (For example, how are toys and play equipment tidied away?)
2   Does the current system help children to get things out easily and put them back?
3   If there are some tasks that children particularly enjoy, can you organise a rota so that there is no argument about whose turn it is?

CASE STUDY

The staff of the Fernton Road after-school club decided that they wanted to involve children more in the running of the club.

They started a Friday afternoon chat session when children could give their opinions about the past week's activities and make suggestions for the next. The staff soon discovered that the children preferred to pick from a list of possibilities, rather than to have the whole responsibility of thinking of what to do. Soon this planning extended to the snack menu as well.

So far the workers had always done the washing-up after snack time. They asked whether any children would like to help. To their surprise, most children wanted to help and a rota had to be organised. The children enjoyed chatting with the worker in charge of washing-up. Workers had to find a set of steps for the smallest child, who refused to be left out.

1   Do you give children tasks to help with the organisation of your nursery or playgroup?
2   Are children resistant to helping with tidying up? Can you make changes that might encourage them? For example, do you leave enough time for a leisurely tidy-up? Do the children have clearly defined tasks?
3   Are you doing some tasks alone that children might enjoy doing with you – for example, reorganising cupboards, simple washing-up, or folding clothes?

2.6 Planning what to do with children

Planning a programme of activities

You should have a plan of what you will do with children, although you will be wise to keep some flexibility within this. The goal of any programme for children is to help them learn and progress in all the areas of their development.

Your final decisions about what to do will depend, of course, on the age of the children in your care, their range of abilities and the setting in which you are working. How much choice you offer will depend on the number of children for whom you are responsible.

Many activities will help children learn in more than one way. For example, children enjoy dancing as a lively physical activity, but it is also a way of expressing themselves. Additionally, they can develop an enjoyment and appreciation of different kinds of music. Playing with sand or water is a satisfying physical experience of feeling; children may also learn some basic scientific ideas from handling these materials. And these can also be a source of imaginative play.

Check that the range of activities you offer can support children in all of the following.

Physical development

- Using their whole bodies in climbing and running, playing physical games indoors and outside.
- Using their hands in building and craft activities.

Communication

- An opportunity to communicate through gestures, touch and words.
- Talking and listening as individuals and in groups.
- Experiencing books and other written material.
- Self-expression through dance and drama.
- Conversation to explain and explore ideas and opinions.

Self-help and responsibility

- Learning how to take care of themselves and to be involved in everyday tasks.

Imagination and creativity

- Opportunities and play materials to exercise the imagination.
- A wide range of craft materials and help to learn skills to stretch creative expression.

Understanding ideas and the world around them

- Exploring basic ideas of science and mathematics through play materials.
- Trips out, books and other materials to extend understanding of the world.

If you are working in schools then the requirements of the National Curriculum will influence the programme of activities. There is a reference at the end of this section for you to find out more.

Helping children learn

In anything that you plan to do with children, remember the following important points about how children learn.

Remembering

An essential part of learning information or skills is remembering. You will help children by bearing in mind the other points that follow, such as helping them notice and giving them practice. You can also help children directly by:

- remembering together, through talking about outings and activities you have shared with children;
- choosing play activities that combine new with familiar toys and games;

- being prepared to repeat information or instructions, and encouraging children to repeat these back to you when appropriate;
- playing games that specifically encourage remembering – round games like 'I went to the shops and I bought . . .' or card games like 'pairs'.

Noticing

Children will not remember something that they scarcely noticed or heard in the first place. You can help them:

- by showing children how *you* look carefully and listen;
- by pointing out events of interest and by playing 'spotting' games (looking at a picture, or when you are on a trip);
- by taking notice when children want you to look at something which interests them.

Feeling confident

If children lack confidence in themselves they may not even attempt something: they may give up before they start.

You can help children keep trying with your encouragement:

- be generous with your compliments about what they have done and how they have done it;
- help them to complete something to their own satisfaction, but try not to take over;
- help them to learn from what has gone wrong as well as from what has gone right – mistakes or frustrations can be a source of learning for children, if you help them to see these that way;
- remind children of the things they have learned.

Practising

Children need to practise a skill or rehearse new knowledge if they are to be confident in their learning. You can explain to children that everyone has to practise.

You can help them by encouraging them to persevere with learning a skill, like doing up buttons or crayoning, until it feels easier. Children who are learning to read or to understand how to do sums need a lot of practice; any such practice is over a period of time.

A confident builder

Evaluating programmes

Every now and then, make a quiet time and think about what you do with children. These are some questions that you could ask yourself or talk over with fellow workers.

Do I undervalue any potential area of play?

For example, do you join in with children in their outdoor play? They would probably enjoy this sometimes.

Am I making unhelpful distinctions?

For instance, are you taking an adult view of play? Babies and toddlers will enjoy times of physical care for them if you make these times of closeness and affectionate communication.

Do I ignore any source of play materials?

For instance, have you dismissed the fact that you yourself are an immensely valuable toy? You are a rich source of language experiences – conversation, story times, joke times. Your body is a vital piece of equipment for babies, toddlers and young children. They will relish having you to crawl over and jump on.

Am I encouraging children to do real cooking, real tidying, real shopping?

They love 'pretend' play and acting out scenes from the adult world. However, they do not need to experience this world only through toys.

Do I ask the children for their opinions?

If asked, most 3- and 4-year-olds will tell you what they enjoyed; it will become obvious also from their conversation which activities they remember. This will give you some idea about whether activities are working as you intended.

Choosing play materials

Whatever your work setting, you need to ask yourself some questions about the play materials that you have and any that you plan to buy. Any materials that you use must be safe and in good condition. When you consider buying any more toys or equipment, you also want good value for money.

Safety

Are toys strong enough for the amount of use they are likely to get? Check regularly that equipment is in good repair: there should not be bits about to fall off or sharp edges. If you are responsible for buying equipment choose from reputable firms and, if at all possible, select material that has the British Standard kitemark.

Babies need toys different from those of older children

A certain amount depends on the age of the children. Younger children will put objects in their mouths. A constructional set with very small pieces would not be suitable for a 1-year-old, yet could be both safe and challenging for a 5-year-old. Baby toys might be quite safe for 4-year-olds but will not interest them for long.

You also need to keep play materials well organised. Check that bits of puzzles are not lost. Try to keep different kinds of building material stored together. Make sure that craft materials are cleaned up and put away carefully. Involve the children, even young ones, in keeping the play materials tidy and well organised.

A good range

Does an expensive piece of equipment offer an extension to the kind of play available to children? You need materials that can be put together to help all aspects of children's development. They are developing physically at the same time as they progress intellectually and develop socially.

What kind of world?

All kinds of play material communicate a message to children about the world as a whole and about the place of individual children within the world.

Take a careful look at the toys that you have, the selection of books and the posters on the wall. What image of the world emerges from the play materials that you use? Does this image reflect the children's immediate environment and also settings which are less familiar to them?

You need to concern yourself with how different races are shown through the play materials, regardless of the racial mix of the children attending your workplace. If you work in an all-black school in an all-black area, or an all-white nursery in an all-white area, bear in mind that play materials and illustrations may be the children's main source of ideas about other races.

All children have the right to see other children and adults like themselves in stories and in wall posters. The characters portrayed should sometimes be central, not always minor, figures in a story. Wall posters should include adults of varied races, and with and without disabilities, in a range of jobs.

It is very important that boys and girls can see themselves portrayed positively in books and illustrations. Do the books that you read have heroines as well as heroes?

Have you any illustrations of children with disabilities in everyday situations? It can be emotionally damaging to a child with disabilities if she never sees a character like herself as someone important in a story, or disabled characters are portrayed only as the objects of pity.

Reading on . . .

Chapters 4, 5 and 6 of the workbook offer many ideas about activities suitable for different levels and areas of child development. If you want more information, the guidelines given in section 2.1 will be useful. You can add also:

★ Gillespie, John 1992: *Parents' Curriculum Guide*, 3rd edn (W. H. Smith Exclusive Books).

★ National Children's Bureau 1989: *Working With Children: developing a curriculum for the early years.*

2.7 Observation, assessment and record-keeping

Our aim in this section is to look broadly at the process of observation and assessment. We cover:

- reasons for observing;
- how to plan and carry out different kinds of observations;
- important issues in interpreting observations;
- key concerns in writing down observations and conclusions.

This section will be important for you in your work whether or not you use prepared material like guides. At root, observation involves watching and listening; assessment consists of coming to conclusions on the basis of your observations. Every worker does this, even if in the most informal way.

Why observe?

The first answer to this question is that you cannot help but observe because you'll watch and listen to what goes on: you won't be able to stop yourself. Good practice in work with the under-8s includes developing the habit of being observant.

You need to keep alert to the children during the usual course of a day. You will have impressions of what children did, memories of what you did and a feel about how it all went. If you work with another adult, you can pool your impressions and learn a lot from this.

However, working with babies and children is hard work. You will not notice everything; some days your attention will be caught by more dramatic events or by particular children. For this reason you will find it useful to gather information on children in a more organised way and on a regular basis. You are making these more formal observations *as well as* being alert – not instead of this.

There will probably be three main reasons for you to plan an observation:

- to gain a full picture of an individual child – what she can do and what she can't yet do;
- if you are concerned about a child's development or behaviour, to look for patterns that will help you to help the child;
- to get a reliable picture of how children are using, or not using, certain activities or equipment.

Objectivity is important

Observations are based on the evidence of your senses, mainly:

- What have you seen?
- What have you heard?

However, the nature of human perception is that we all try to make sense of what we have observed almost as fast as we are observing it: you will not be able entirely to stop yourself from this. Your responsibility is to remain as fully aware as possible of how your own assumptions are shaping what you have seen and heard. If you work well with co-workers you will be able to help each other.

At the simplest level, we all interpret what we see

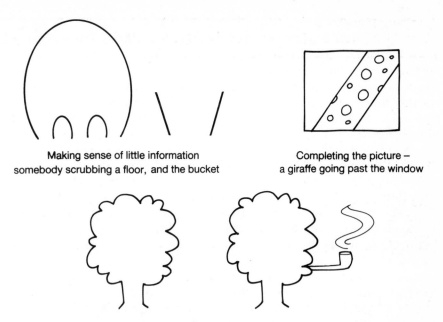

Making sense of little information
somebody scrubbing a floor, and the bucket

Completing the picture –
a giraffe going past the window

A few more lines – from a tree to someone smoking a pipe

It takes practice to notice the difference between your actual observations and:

- what you *expected* to see or hear;
- what you *hoped* you would see or hear;
- your interpretations and guesses about what is going on and why.

There is nothing the matter with having expectations or hopes – these are inevitable. There is nothing wrong with making sense of your observations; this is an important step for you to take. However, you need to be able to unravel them from the actual observations.

Common mistakes

Jumping to conclusions
Example In a playgroup, both Darren and Fiona are wearing thin shoes on a cold day. The worker's expectations of the two different families encourage her to believe that Darren's parents were simply in a hurry, whereas she becomes even more convinced that Fiona's parents neglect her.
Comment The worker may be right, at least in part – but she is running the risk of reinforcing unwarranted assumptions by interpreting similar events in very different ways, depending on her existing view of the families involved.

Over-generalising
Example In a nursery group, 3-year-old Lee is stamping and shouting as he waits for his morning drink. One worker comments to another that Lee is 'always so impatient'.
Comment Again, the workers may have a point. However, they are generalising from Lee's behaviour in one particular situation to make an all-inclusive criticism of his personality. Words like 'always', 'never' or 'typical' are seldom useful or accurate terms.

Guessing feelings

Example   George's mother never stays more than a few minutes when she drops him at playgroup. The workers conclude that she doesn't care; they say that she just 'dumps' George.

Comment   There could be a number of reasons why George's mother does not stay long in playgroup. She may be in a hurry to meet other commitments. She may not feel welcome in the group. Or she may have learned from experience that if she stays for any length of time, George will not let her go at all. The playgroup workers cannot come to any fair conclusions about her feelings without more information, including talking with her.

Labelling

Example   In a day nursery, 4-year-old Rafat can complete the most difficult jigsaws in the toy box; the workers say he is 'bright'. On several occasions 4-year-old Janice has been seen hitting a younger child; the workers say she is a 'bully'.

Comment   Each of these words is dangerous shorthand for a description of *behaviour*, not of the *person*. Neither is very useful without more information, even though the workers would feel they were being complimentary to Rafat.

How to be more objective

You can be appropriately objective in what you make of your informal everyday observations. The same guidelines apply for any of the more organised observations of children or activities.

Describe behaviour and events that you have actually observed

Avoid shorthand labels, even if they aren't criticisms. This applies to what you say as well as what you write.

Instead, describe what you have seen and how children or adults have behaved. What did they do? What did they say? What happened?

Your opinions are valuable – but you may be mistaken

Present your opinions honestly as such, not as proven facts. By all means share your opinions, but start with words like 'I think that . . .' or 'It seems to me that . . .' Then support your opinions with your reasons; the word 'because' has to follow.

Sometimes you will have to think quite hard to identify your reasons. Perhaps you have a 'feel' about a child or a family. If you have developed this feel from what you have observed, you'll be able to track it down. If you fail to do this, question whether your gut feeling is based on unsupported assumptions or prejudices about a child or family.

Any observation is selective

You have watched or heard a child at a particular time in a particular place. There are some practical ideas later in this section to deal with the issue of observation as only a part of the whole picture.

You should try to make sense of any observation, however you do it. To place what you have observed in context, you need:

- a knowledge of the individual child whom you are observing;
- a knowledge of children in general – their development and usual range of behaviour;
- an awareness of the time and place of your observation.

Planned observations

Sometimes you will set out to undertake an observation of an individual child or a group. You may use a prepared plan for what you will observe or a list of items that you want to check. There are a number of different approaches that you might take.

All the comments made so far in this section apply to any of these methods. Any observation – or any test, for that matter – can only be as good as the person using it and his or her caution in generalising from the information.

Developmental guides

How this can help

A prepared guide to developmental stages and steps can help you assess the current abilities of an individual child. From this you can plan to give the most appropriate attention to meet the needs of the individual child. A guide should also help you to pinpoint any problems within a child's development.

You usually gather your information over a short period of time. You combine observation of children's spontaneous play with setting up play situations to observe what children can manage.

Some guides provide a selection of items that relate to children's development in the different areas; usually you tick whether children can or can't yet do something. There may also be space for descriptive comments. One example is the Portage Early Education Programme Checklist, published by NFER/Nelson.

An alternative style is for a guide to offer a series of headings. You then describe a child's abilities and interests under each heading. An example of this approach is Sheila Wolfendale's *All About Me*, published by Nottingham Educational Supplies.

Turning the tables on the adults

Basic do's and don'ts

Whatever the exact layout that you are using in your work, there are some consistent guidelines for good practice.

Assess what a child can manage now without your hints and promptings

Don't muddle up this activity with helping a child to learn. You may also have to discourage other children from giving prompts if you are observing within a busy room.

This warning is particularly important when you are observing a child's language or understanding of ideas. Explain to the child that, 'This time I want to see what you can do by yourself.'

On the other hand, it doesn't matter if you demonstrate a physical skill, like hopping, and ask 'Can you do that?' You are interested in whether the child is physically *able* to hop, not whether she understands the word.

Give the child your full attention throughout the observation

Be ready to settle her into what you want her to try. Don't ask a question and then turn away.

Don't alter the questions or instructions from a developmental guide . . .

Sometimes this might not matter too much, but at others you might inadvertently change the real question that you are asking. Or you might give help in a way that would confuse your assessment.

. . . But don't use items that are clearly inappropriate

For example, it is only sensible to consider whether a child has the physical dexterity to eat using a knife and fork if this is the usual way that his family eats.

Don't coach children to 'pass' particular items in a guide or checklist

Practical lessons from any observation and assessment should broaden out from the particular areas in which a child has done well or not so well.

Using the information

You can make sense of this kind of observation in two ways:

- *Making a direct comparison between a child now and how she was a few months or a year ago*   In effect, this takes two snapshots of the same child and asks: 'In what way has she changed?'

- *Comparing this child with a group of similar children (usually children of a similar age)*   This answers the question: 'How is she developing compared with the others?'

The first approach can tell you how much a child's hard work has paid off. For example, 'Sonia got over her nervousness about the climbing frame. She clambers up confidently to the top now.' Or it may warn you that a child has hardly changed over months – 'Nicky is still as confused about counting as he was last January. We need to rethink how we are helping him on this.'

The second approach tells you how children are doing compared with an average for the age group. Averages in development are always about age ranges, not exact age in years and months.

Some people worry that children will be labelled or will be upset if they feel less able than others. This *can* happen if workers go against all the guidelines on objectivity given earlier: it is not inevitable, however. Look also at 'Talking with children' which comes later in this section.

Focused observation of play and behaviour

All observations are selective in one way or another. You see a bit of the picture, not all of it. There are a number of practical ways of taking a sample from all the possible material that you could observe. Here we are describing these ideas very briefly: the suggested reading at the end of the section gives a lot more detail.

Observing children's climbing skills

Short bursts of observation

It is not possible to sit for long stretches of time attempting to note down everything that happens. If you try this, you won't be able to make much sense of what you have at the end.

The practical alternative is to take samples: short bursts of time spread over a longer total period. Decide where you want to focus your attention and give yourself a realistic pattern for observing.

In most of these examples, you will need a stopwatch or at least a watch with a clear minute indicator. It is worth laying out your sheet of paper by times and headings before you start.

Carry out any observation at least three or four times over a week or two. You are trying to make sure that your observations do not by chance pick up a day that is not at all typical of how the children usually behave. Activities 1 and 2 illustrate ways of sampling time.

Focus on behaviour

Sometimes it will make more sense to put your full attention onto one particular kind of behaviour. In practice you will probably only do this when you are worried or frustrated by a child's behaviour; however, you could make this kind of observation for any behaviour. Activity 3 illustrates this kind of approach.

In section 7.2 there is more about looking for patterns in children's behaviour.

Using observations

Each of the activities is followed by some questions. In general terms, you will always be thinking about what you can learn from the observation. If you were concerned about a problem, is it as serious as you thought? Can you see patterns in what is happening? What can you do on the basis of what you have learned? (You are *never* asking the question of who is to blame.)

Keeping records

Prompt writing up

In any of the focused observation methods described earlier, note down as you observe. Your more informal observations day by day should be written down as soon as possible.

The longer you leave it, the less reliable any notes will be. So as well as giving the date and time of any observation, you should also write down when you made the notes. Give the name of the child or children, and your own name as the person who made the observation.

Make it legible

It may seem obvious, but do make your notes easy to read. Today's shorthand can be tomorrow's illegible squiggle. Whenever possible make life easier for yourself by having prepared sheets: it's a waste of precious time to keep writing out the same headings.

Separate your observation from your interpretation

Even if you are writing very short reports, do make separate sections for:

- *your observations* – what you saw or heard, your description of events;
- *the sense you make of your observations* – supported by your reasons;
- *any conclusions or recommendations.*

All the guidelines for objectivity given at the beginning of this section apply equally strongly to written material on children or families.

Confidentiality and access

Your own personal jottings are confidential to you. However, it is still inappropriate to write down anything that you would be embarrassed for someone else to see.

It is good practice that reports on children should be made available to their parents. Check on the exact procedure in your place of work. Whatever this is, you may not make available to parents reports written by other people unless they have given permission. Be honest with a parent about the reason you have to remove a report from their child's folder before showing it.

Make sure that people who have no business looking at children's folders cannot glance through them. Ideally, store all reports in a locked cabinet or cupboard.

ACTIVITY 1

Observation of children in the home corner
You might be interested in how children use the home corner.

Select an hour of the day when you are likely to be able to watch without too many distractions. One possibility is to focus your full attention on the home corner every five minutes. You watch for a minute, noting as you go; you stop watching at the end of the minute and can complete your notes in the four minutes before you focus on the home corner once again.

Decide what questions you would like to explore and lay out headings or boxes on paper to help you. It might look something like the example on the right.

First note down the information that you most want to know – perhaps you are especially interested in which children use the home corner, how many of them are boys and how many girls, and what games they play with the material in the corner. Write anything else that you have time to get down from what children say to each other and how they use the materials.

DATE: 27/4/93   YOUR NAME: Andy

TIME:	CHILDREN'S NAMES:	ACTIVITY:
10.00	Sasha & Damien Ray	Tea party Putting baby doll to bed.

COMMENTS: Damien seems to be leading the tea party, telling Sasha how to make the tea and what plates to get out. Sasha calls to Emma to come and join them. Ray very careful with the baby, tucks it up several times till he looks satisfied. Kisses the doll on the nose.

10.05   ...
10.10   ...

ACTIVITY 2

Observation of how an individual child uses his time

You might be concerned to find out how Daniel spends his time in your group. Perhaps you think he only plays with a very narrow range of toys or you are worried that he does not seem to play with any other children.

You could decide to look at Daniel at regular intervals throughout part of the day or session and repeat this observation over a few days. You wish to check whether your impression is accurate and look for any patterns that could help you to work with him.

For instance, you might make sure that at every half-hour and hour you note down what Daniel is doing and who his companions are, if he has any. There is no need to write a long report each time: just describe briefly what you can observe. Your prepared sheet might look something like the one on the right.

If you do this for at least several days, you should gain a fairly reliable picture of the ways in which Daniel spends his time. On the basis of your information you can come to a careful assessment. Does Daniel seem to have any friends? Does he appear to know how to approach other children in a friendly way? Is he a child who warms up as the day progresses? Does he need your help?

DATE: 10/2/93   YOUR NAME: Jessica

TIME: 2.00   CHILD'S NAME: Daniel

D. standing by the window. Seems to be watching the birds. Waves his hand. Nobody with him.

2.30

D. watching Freddy, John and Asif at the building table. They are busy. D. appears to move to sit down but then stops.

3.00

Daniel at the sand tray beside Valerie. She is making sand shapes. D. goes to take the little bucket. V. says 'No, in a minute!'

ACTIVITY 3

Observation of a child's behaviour

Sometimes you want to get an accurate view of what a child is doing. You are interested in, or concerned about, a particular way of behaving.

The first step is to describe clearly for yourself the behaviour that you want to observe. You need to get beyond the shorthand label.

You might say that Grace is 'disruptive'. But what does she actually do? Perhaps she grabs books or toys that other children are using. Perhaps she is also unable to sit still at story time, and pokes other children or fidgets.

Now you can observe Grace over a period of several days and simply note down how often she behaves in this way. Make sure that any co-workers who take over observing are using your definition of 'disruptive'. Your observation could look like the record sheet shown.

Once you have a week or so of observations, you may be able to see a pattern. Does Grace provoke some children more than others? Is story time less of a problem than you anticipated? (Perhaps it's just that it's particularly annoying when she disturbs that activity.) Have you seen any hints of how to help Grace – can she be distracted from the grabbing, does she need support in learning how to play?

CHILD'S NAME: Grace   YOUR NAME: Teja

DATE	Grabbing toys	Story time	Comment
Wed. 5/5/93	**	*	G. took books from Jason each time. Poked Anneka during story.
Thurs. 6/5/93	***	–	Took Rachel's bricks for her building, twice. Then ran off with Jason's favourite bike.
Fri. 7/5/93	*	–	Fight in home corner over a toy kettle.

Talking about observations and assessments

With co-workers

It will be helpful to share information and ideas with your co-workers. An open discussion could also help you sort out whether prior assumptions are colouring how you interpret your observations, or whether your frustrations with a child are getting in the way of finding a way to help him.

Obviously for any discussion to work all those involved need to support each other's efforts and to express any potential criticism in the most constructive ways.

With parents

In your earliest conversations with parents, explain the ways that you observe all children in the group. Talk about any written guides or report forms that you use on a regular basis. Section 2.4 has a lot more material about partnership with parents; please use the following suggestions within that context.

Most parents will be interested in the results of any developmental assessment of their child. Share the full picture that has emerged with them. Ask for *their* experience of their child, as well as for their comments on what *you* have observed. You can usefully focus on:

- *the child's current stage of development* and what she can do;
- *how she has changed* since the last full look at her development;
- *what she is nearly able to do* and how best to help her now;
- *whether she has any difficulties* that need special attention or specialist help.

If you have made any observations of children's behaviour then you could share these as well. Perhaps you were observing because you were having difficulties with the child: look at the ideas under 'Difficult conversations' in section 2.4.

With children

What you say and how you say it will depend of course on the age and maturity of the children.

If you have gathered information using a developmental guide of some type, then do consider chatting with the children afterwards. Even 3- and 4-year-olds will have realised that you have been doing some special work and will be interested.

There is no need to give them an exhausting rundown of everything that you have learned. However, you can share some compliments and some insights. For example:

- You might tell 3-year-old David, 'I can see that you can cut now. Well done.' It is important to compliment children for persevering through the difficult stage when they can't make simple tools work for them.
- You could point out to 7-year-old Sasha, 'Have you noticed how easily you can add up now? Do you remember when you told me you'd never ever manage it?' You can help children to realise what they have achieved. Often they can't see beyond the next stage, which is such a struggle at the moment.

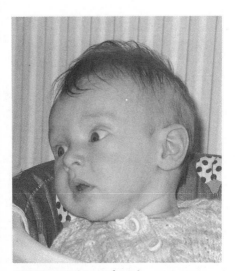

Who's watching whom?

- You need to reassure children that you are trying to help them. For example, you can chat with 4-year-old Peter to explain, 'I think I can see now how you have got confused about colours. Perhaps if we try it this way . . .'

You could share with children ideas that have emerged from your observations of how they use the home corner. Or you could explain the new way that you would like to organise snack-time, which you hope will reduce the chaos of the old system. It may be a revelation to children that adults consider what they do! So why not share the results? 'I've been watching. . . .' 'I've been thinking about. . . .'

Reading on . . .

This section has only touched on some issues in observation and assessment. You can explore the topic further with these books:
★ Drummond, Mary-Jane, Dorothy Rouse and Gillian Pugh 1992: *Making Assessment Work – values and principles in assessing young children's learning* (NCB/NES Arnold).
★ Laishley, Jennie 1987: *Working with Young Children*, Part One (Hodder & Stoughton).
★ Merttens, Ruth and Jeff Vass 1989: *The National Curriculum – a survival guide for parents* (Octopus).

For your information

Two pieces of legislation may affect the kind of formal assessments which need to be done if you are working in a school. You yourself may not be involved in actually carrying out the assessment; however, if you know the child or children, then the teacher or specialist who does carry it out should ask you for your considered opinion.

- *Education Act 1981* This included the plan to have statements of special educational need. Known as 'statementing', this has in practice tended to be for children with disabilities or learning difficulties.

- *Education Reform Act 1988* This set out the National Curriculum and the plan for assessment of schoolchildren at a number of key stages. This assessment is through the Standard Assessment Tasks (SATs).

3 Physical and emotional well-being of children

3.1 Keeping babies and children well and healthy

Caring about children

An integral part of *caring for* children's health, welfare and development is *caring about* them as individuals. It is vital that children should feel confident that people care about them and about what happens to them. You communicate this to children as much through physical care, given with affection, as through your encouragement in the activities that stretch them intellectually.

Remember that children's physical needs are part of a bigger picture of all their needs. The physical care that you give to babies and younger children at meal-time and when changing nappies can also be a time of enjoyment. You can make close individual contact through chatting and smiling.

Don't think of physical care as something that you have to rush through in order to make time for what you see as proper playtime. Babies and young children don't make this sharp distinction: there is no reason for *you* to do so.

Obviously you do need to keep to standards of hygiene in changing babies and young children, and you don't wish children to think of food as a play material. However, you need not allow such standards to make physical care an emotionally cold time. Nor should routines for physical care ever become more important than the children themselves.

Children with disabilities may have special physical needs; these also can be times when you can make personal contact with an individual child. Your sensitivity to a child's feelings will be especially important when she needs help in physical care at an age when her peers can manage alone.

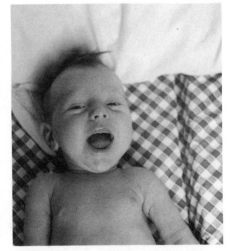

For him, changing time is a chance to chat

Children need touch

Babies and children need physical contact: it is an important channel for warm communication. Contact is also reassuring when children are worried or upset.

Children should be treated with respect. They should not be used as comfort objects. You may have to step in if older children are treating a baby or young child like a doll or as a prop in a game. Equally, it is not acceptable for workers responsible for rather exhausting older groups of children to appear in the baby room for a bit of peace and a baby to cuddle because it makes *them* feel better.

Be alert to a child's feelings. You should not feel hurt if he does not want a cuddle at the moment. Some children like to kiss adults goodbye, but that is *their* choice: you should not insist. Babies, toddlers and children will show when they want physical contact with you by touching you, taking your hand or snuggling up to you.

Children who do not want much closeness may still be pleased for you to be nearby. There are differences between families in the degree of physical affection shown to children. Some of these differences may be cultural, some are more individual family tradition.

You need to be alert to the child who appears to be *unnerved* by physical closeness. She may have had a bad experience. Be alert also to children who have learned inappropriate touching. (You will find more information about child abuse within section 3.5.)

Babies and toddlers do not understand that some areas of the body are viewed as more private. If you are female, you may well find that very young children will idly put a hand down the front of your blouse or dress. You can gently remove the hand. However, older children should not be trying to fondle your breasts if you are female or the crutch area of male or female workers.

Don't stop showing affection to the children just because they are older. Not all 6- and 7-year-olds want a hand held or a lap to sit on, but you can still sit close and show warmth by a brief touch on the arm or the shoulder.

Standards for cleanliness

Clean and tidy

A safe environment for babies and children is free from threats to their physical well-being and health. Their environment should be clean, but cleaning activities should not dominate your day with children.

You need to maintain a level of tidiness such that neither you nor the children trip over things. However, you will have a miserable time with children if you try to maintain neatness at all times. You will need regular tidying-up times throughout a day and your aim is to involve children in this process.

Babies and toddlers need to be kept clean and comfortable. They need cleaning from time to time and one set of clothes is very unlikely to last as long as a day. Older children may make one outfit last for a day, so long as they are equipped with aprons or overalls for painting and similar activities.

Sterilisation and strict hygiene

Feeding and meals

Cleanliness alone is not enough when you are bottle-feeding babies. You must also be exact in following the instructions for mixing milk according to the formula given on the container. Bottles and teats must be sterilised according to the instructions on the products.

Nappies

If a child wears towelling nappies then these must be sterilised before they are washed. Again, you will find clear instructions on products designed for the purpose. If a child wears disposable nappies, then you should place the used nappy in a plastic bag and seal the top before disposing of it.

Changing children, and accidents

You should follow a careful procedure to avoid cross-infection through your contact with any body fluids or body products, whatever the age of the child.

You should wear a fresh pair of disposable plastic gloves every time that you change a child or deal with any accident in which a child's skin is broken. After use the gloves should be placed in a sealed bag, in the same way as a disposable nappy.

These precautions have become good practice for group care in recent years as a response to concerns about conditions such as AIDS and hepatitis. However, you will not necessarily know when a child has these or other infectious conditions. You should therefore use the same precautionary hygiene procedure for every child.

It is safer for you and for the children to treat all body fluids and body products as potentially infectious. It is also kinder to children who are known to have a health problem that they are not visibly being treated differently from other children. Explain simply to any child who asks that you come into contact with so many adults and children that you could pass on germs without meaning to.

Children need opportunities to run about

Rest and sleep

The majority of babies will have daytime sleeps. Children up to 3 and 4 years old may still need a daytime nap; this tends to change into a quiet time rather than actually falling asleep.

You need to be organised so that children who need a nap can rest comfortably and children who are awake can play without disturbing the sleepers. Arrange a quiet time with books or peaceful activities on a table or rug.

Care of babies

Some babies in the early months of life die in their sleep for no obvious reason. This is called 'sudden infant death syndrome' or 'cot death'. There is still no clear explanation of why this happens and it may be that there is no single cause.

In 1992, the Foundation for the Study of Infant Deaths (FSID) was making the following recommendations. You should be ready to check on current advice as it emerges.

Place babies on their back or their side to sleep

In the 1980s parents were told not to place babies on their backs, for fear of choking. This is not now regarded as a risk. Sometimes doctors may recommend that a baby lies on the stomach for medical reasons, in which case you need to check that the clothes do not cover the baby completely.

Do not use pillows with babies under 12 months old

The FSID also suggests not using duvets, baby nests, cot bumpers or sheepskins. There is concern that babies may get entangled in this kind of bedding or get too hot.

Avoid smoking and smoky atmospheres

Breathing becomes more difficult in a smoky environment and can be especially hard if babies get colds. It is not, of course, good practice to smoke in the same room as children of any age.

Do not let babies get too hot or too cold

Babies should not be left to sleep outside for long periods, especially in cooler weather. If it is suitable for them to nap outside, then you should stay close by and check them regularly.

Babies can also get overheated and this may be a factor in some unexplained deaths. Young babies need to be warmly dressed until they get better at keeping themselves warm. On the other hand, the FSID suggests that babies of a month and over, whilst they are indoors, do not need more layers of clothes than does the adult caring for them. Even younger babies do not need a lot more than this.

Babies need protection from draughts and more layers than walking adults when they are taken out in a pram or buggy. However, outdoor clothes should be removed when a sleeping baby or child is brought inside.

Babies do not need hot rooms – about 65 °F (18 °C) is fine – nor do they need to be put next to radiators or other sources of direct heat.

Babies should not normally sweat, feel hot to your touch, or get heat rashes in cool weather. You can check whether they are comfortably warm by slipping your hand inside their clothes and feeling their stomach. They should feel warm but not hot.

Contact the doctor if babies are unwell

This may be just for advice or you may want the doctor to see the baby. Remember that babies who have a high temperature need less clothes or bedding, not more.

For your information

For further advice, contact the Foundation for the Study of Infant Deaths: 35 Belgrave Square, London SW1X 8QB (*tel.* 071–235 0965; helpline: 071–235 1721).

Reading on . . .

If you are working with children into the evening or overnight, you may be facing problems with children who won't settle. They may wake at night and then wake you as well. These two books offer some practical suggestions:
★   Haslam, David 1984: *Sleepless Children* (Piatkus).
★   Douglas, Jo and Naomi Richman 1984: *My Child Won't Sleep* (Penguin).

3.2 A healthy diet

This is an area in which you will not be short of advice! Every few weeks, it seems, a newspaper or magazine article gives new rules about diet or overturns old ones. In fact, the basic questions are as they have always been:

- Are children eating an adequate amount of food and drinking enough liquid in total – not too much or too little?
- Are they eating and drinking a healthy balance between different kinds of food and drink?

There are few, if any, foods that are absolutely good or bad: the problems come more from badly unbalanced diets. For instance, carrots are a nutritious food but you will be ill if you eat them in ludicrously large quantities.

Different diets

Around the world a family's diet is influenced by cultural tradition and any religious considerations. Your own view of a normal diet will have been influenced by your own upbringing. Don't view a diet as 'restricted' just because it doesn't include foods that *you* happily eat.

You may encounter a number of different diets. Remember that there are different routes to achieving a balanced and therefore a healthy diet.

Diets with meat

Families who eat meat as part of their diet do not usually eat every possible kind of meat – some avoid particular animals for religious reasons or require that the animals be killed in a particular way.

Packed lunches can be nutritious too

Some families have preferences based on national tradition. For example, English families might be outraged at the suggestion that they eat horse, yet this is a possibility in parts of mainland Europe. In turn some European countries think it very odd to eat lamb – a traditional meat in England and Greece.

Vegetarian

Strictly speaking, vegetarians will not eat any food that requires the killing of any animal, including poultry and fish. If you are planning menus for children who are vegetarian you need to get into the habit of checking the ingredients on convenience foods – for example, some ice cream includes animal fat. You should also use vegetarian cheeses since most cheese is made with rennet, which is derived from animals.

However, some families who describe themselves as vegetarian eat fish or are not that concerned about ingredients in convenience foods. As with any other practical issue, check with parents so that you understand what they want for their child.

Vegan

A vegan diet excludes any food that comes from animals, however humanely it may be produced. Vegans will not drink milk or eat other dairy produce. They do not eat eggs, and some vegans avoid honey.

A balanced vegan diet needs careful attention, especially if you are not used to this way of eating. For example:

- *Vitamin B12*   Adults and children may need a supplement for vitamin B12. This is largely found in animal products with only traces in sea vegetables (edible seaweeds).
- *Calcium*   Babies and young children who are not yet on a very mixed diet may need a calcium supplement. Soya bean milk is sometimes fortified with calcium.
- *Fat*   There are only traces of fat in fruit and vegetables, so you will need other sources of fat, such as all kinds of nuts and soya flour.

Balanced diets

We haven't given you sample menus: these would take up many pages if we tried to offer all the necessary alternatives. What we *have* done is to summarise for you the practical issues that you should consider. In doing this we have combined the advice given in the books we suggest at the end of this section with that given in general books recommended in other parts of this workbook.

Drinks

Children need liquid from different sources. These can include water, milk (cow's or soya), and fruit or vegetable juices. They should not have lots of drinks with sugar added or squashes. Don't overdo the fruit juice either, since unfortunately teeth do not distinguish between the sugar naturally present in fruit juice and that added to squashes.

Foods

Your task will be easier if you work from four main groupings of food. Menus should include foods from each of the four groups every day. Children, like adults, need variety in their diet, so it is important that you don't always choose the same foods from each group. Some foods, such as cheese or beans, fit into more than one group because of the mixture of nutrients they contain.

Sources of carbohydrates

Carbohydrates occur as sugars and starches. Some foods in this group are also a useful source of fibre. You can choose from:

- all the different kinds of (leavened) bread and rolls;
- different unleavened breads, like chapatis or puris;
- cereals, beans and lentils;
- dishes made from maize, millet and cornmeal;
- noodles and pasta;
- plantains and green bananas;
- potatoes;
- rice;
- sweet potatoes.

Children need sugar as well, but this occurs naturally in many fruits, both fresh and dried. Sugar or honey is also an ingredient in cakes and biscuits. Don't try to remove all sugar, but don't allow sweet foods to dominate a diet or to become important as treats.

Sources of protein

Some foods provide protein in a form that can be fully used by the body even when that food is eaten by itself. These are called 'complete proteins'. The following foods are a good source of complete proteins:

- milk and cheese;
- eggs;
- fish;
- meat;
- poultry.

With the exception of soya beans, plant proteins are 'incomplete proteins'. To provide a complete source of protein they must be eaten in combination with each other. Choose from:

- cereals;
- chickpeas;
- lentils;
- nuts (but don't give these loose to young children, especially the under-3s, because of the danger of choking);
- beans.

Combine these with each other or with the sources of complete protein – for example, beans on toast, millet milk pudding, rice and lentils, breakfast cereal with milk, bread and cheese or hummus (chickpeas and sesame seeds). You can try textured vegetable protein (TVP) and Quorn as alternatives to meat, however these may not be palatable to vegetarians. The very fact that these products are made to look rather like meat can be off-putting.

Fats

Fats are necessary to healthy eating: children won't get a balanced diet if their fat intake is severely reduced. They can get fats in their diet from:

- meat and poultry;
- dairy produce, including cheese, milk, yoghurt and fromage frais;
- nuts (not loose for young children);
- fats as ingredients in cakes, biscuits and pastries.

Children's diet will become unbalanced if any of the foods above dominate meal-times and snacks. Remember that you should be taking foods from each of the four groupings.

Dairy products often come in low-fat versions: use these sparingly. Under-5s, and particularly under-2s, should have full-cream milk, not skimmed.

Watch that you do not add more fat than is needed – fruit and puddings do not necessarily need cream; butter does not have to be spread thickly.

In cooking, use vegetable oils rather than lard and dripping. If some children are vegetarian, it is unacceptable anyway for them to have food that has been cooked with animal fats. Try grilling rather than frying and some foods won't need more oil.

Vitamins and minerals

Choose from the selection of vegetables, fruit and salad stuff that is available. If you live in a city, especially in a racially mixed area, there may be a very good choice available.

Children will get the best from this food if they eat what they enjoy in its raw state. Fruit, carrots, peas, salad vegetables and white cabbage can be served sliced, chopped or grated in an attractive array.

When you boil fruit and vegetables, many of the minerals and vitamins end up in the cooking water. It is therefore a good idea to cook fruit and vegetables lightly in small amounts of water, or to steam them. Use the vegetable water the same day to make sauces or soups, then you aren't pouring nutrients down the drain. Go easy on added salt or sugar. Don't add bicarbonate of soda to keep the colour of vegetables – it destroys vitamin C.

Working with parents on diet

You may be working with a group of children and families whose diets are very diverse. For example, some may be vegetarian while others are meat-eating, and even among those who eat meat there may be different religious requirements about what it may be or how it is to be prepared. An alternative is to offer a non-meat diet. We worked with a community nursery in South London that did this; parents accepted the reasons for the menus offered when these were explained to them.

Ask parents for recipes to help you. If you know very little about a particular diet, the parents may be your best source of information.

Parents may be able to send some food in for their children: if you realistically cannot produce food prepared in the correct way, this may be the best alternative. For example, kosher food simply cannot be produced in a non-kosher kitchen. Parents could provide particular foods for their child if she is allergic to an ingredient that appears in many recipes. For example, some children are made seriously ill by the gluten in flour and need biscuits or cakes made without this.

Don't expect babies to be neat eaters

Read on . . .

For more information try this booklet:

★   Health Education Authority 1991: *Enjoy Healthy Eating*.

There are many cookery books that include meat and vegetarian recipes. The following will help if you want to provide a healthy vegetarian diet or options:

★   Brown, Sarah 1984: *Vegetarian Cookbook* (Dorling Kindersley). As well as recipes, this book has a good section on different sources of nutrients.
★   Canter, David and others 1985: *The Cranks Recipe Book* (Grafton Books). The writers have had experience of running a restaurant. A lot of the recipes are useful if you need to produce food in quantity.

Two series for children will give them and you some information and a few recipes.

★   'Exploring Food in Britain' – a series published by Mantra Publishing.
★   'Food and Drink' – a series published by Wayland.

For your information: religious beliefs and diet

Some religions specify certain diets; you should know about these in order to plan menus for children.

Most of the major world faiths have different sects, and these may differ in their beliefs about diet. Some families follow dietary rules more strictly then others. What follows is therefore only an approximate guide.

● *Buddhists* are often vegetarian but not necessarily – some sects believe diet is a personal decision.

● *Christians* do not all express religious beliefs that influence their diet. Some, however, may choose to eat more simply or to avoid meat on particular days.

● *Hindus* may be vegetarian. Even if their diet includes meat, they do not eat beef in any form.

● *Jehovah's Witnesses* require that meat be killed in a special way, so that it is bled. They do not eat blood products like black pudding.

● *Jews* do not eat pork in any form and often do not eat shellfish either. If families observe the laws of Kashrus, they follow a kosher diet: meat has to be killed in a special way so that it is bled; meat products must be kept separate from dairy products at all stages of food preparation, eating and cleaning up.

● *Mormons* eat meat and meat products, with the exception of foods like black pudding. They avoid caffeine in any form and so avoid tea, coffee or coke drinks.

● *Muslims* do not eat pork in any form and eat only halal meat or poultry. (*Halal* means 'lawful'.) This has been specially killed so that it is bled and dedicated to Allah by a Muslim.

● *Rastafarians* may follow a vegetarian diet close to vegan. If they eat meat, their diet will probably exclude pork and shellfish.

● *Sikhs* are sometimes vegetarian. If they eat meat, then it must *not* have been bled. Sikhs will probably not eat beef or pork.

For your information: food problems

Some children need to avoid certain foods in order to stay well. Talk with parents at the beginning of your working relationship and find out what this means for their child's diet.

Food allergies

This reaction is caused by mechanisms within the body's immune system. If you eat a food to which you are allergic, you will be ill quickly. The food may produce skin rashes, very bad stomach upsets or more violent reactions.

Some children are allergic to egg, wheat, cow's milk, nuts or fish. The milk and egg allergies sometimes pass as children get older; in other cases allergies may last a lifetime.

Food intolerance

Some adverse reactions to foods are less obvious and can be difficult to prove. For example, some children seem to be intolerant of milk, wheat, caffeine, citrus fruits, chocolate, dairy products, and food additives including some colourings. These are said to cause rashes, stomach upsets, migraine and some behaviour changes like hyperactivity or aggression.

Follow the dietary requests that parents ask of you. If you have difficulty maintaining a balanced diet then get them to help you, perhaps by sending in some foods with their children.

3.3 Teaching children to look after themselves

You are starting the process of teaching the under-8s to be able to take care of themselves. They become physically more able to do this and with your encouragement they are pleased with their growing abilities.

The process may be slower if you are working with children with physical disabilities. There may also be a real limit to how much a child can manage without discreet help from you.

Teaching the rules of safety

General safety

Children learn some realities of safety the hard way by banging their heads or hitting their hands. You cannot prevent them hurting themselves altogether, though you can alert them and remind them.

Most 2- and 3-year-olds will learn to follow your cautionary warnings because they trust you. So long as you don't nag or shout, they will listen. However, they have only a limited understanding of your worries for them.

As 4-year-olds and older they will begin to grasp your reasons for saying 'don't' or 'watch out'. However, you have to be ready to repeat your warnings and your reasons.

Don't be surprised if they fail to make a danger link which seems obvious to you. For example, they may have learned that boiling water is potentially dangerous, but they will not immediately make the link to steam. Even 5- and 6-year-olds can be very literal; your warnings about the dangers of one stretch of water may not be generalised to any other river or lake.

Look at section 6.1 to remind yourself of how children of different ages understand the world.

Road safety

You ensure the safety of young children by having them secure in buggies or holding your hand. See section 2.5 for more on safety.

You can use books and posters to supplement what you teach children through words. However, children will learn best through safe practice with you, and with their parents. Use trips out to teach practical skills for crossing roads and awareness of traffic. Don't expect even the 6- and 7-year-olds to be totally reliable.

Personal safety

You can begin to teach children of about 4 years old some basic rules of personal safety. However, you should discuss this with parents before you start; the rules that you teach children are not only about danger from strangers.

You cannot teach children personal safety in one telling. You must build up for them an understanding of considerate and proper behaviour towards children. You can teach them some basics of taking care of themselves and how to handle worrying situations like getting lost.

All children need to understand their basic rights of personal safety. These are summed up by saying:

- *The right to say no*   The child's body belongs to her. She has the right to say 'No' to any adult or child who touches her in a way that she does not want.
- *The right to tell*   If anybody refuses to take notice when a child says 'No', then he can then tell on that person.
- *The right not to keep secrets*   Children need to be encouraged not to keep a secret that does not feel right.
- *The right not to be bound by social rules*   Reassure children that if adults do not behave properly, then the usual politeness rules don't apply.

Be careful, though, to avoid any implied message to children that they are totally responsible for keeping themselves safe from harm. If they feel they have permission to shout and run away from strangers who behave inappropriately, they may be able to get themselves out of some situations. But this will not be the case when adults use their greater strength, or when familiar adults and teenagers abuse their closeness to children. It is bad enough that the children are hurt or frightened; they must not also be left feeling at fault because they could not save themselves.

Children need to feel sure that troubles with an adult or child, even from within the family, can be reported to a parent or other trusted adult and that they will be believed. We talk about this issue in section 3.5.

Reading on . . .

The introductions to some of these books will help you to be positive in how you express the ideas to children. You do not want to give them the impression that there are dangerous adults lurking behind every bush.
★   The 'Watch Out' series published by Wayland has simple text and illustrations to explain dangers.
★   For stories and pictures with the under-5s, try Michele Elliott's *Feeling Happy, Feeling Safe* (Hodder & Stoughton, 1991).
★   For the over-5s, see Michele Elliott's *The Willow Street Kids* (Piccolo, 1987).
★   Kidscape has a good selection of posters and books for this topic. Contact them at the World Trade Centre, Europe House, London E1 9AA (*tel.* 071–488 2400).

Helping out

Young children enjoy learning some of the simpler tasks of running everyday life. Tasks that seem dull or very routine to you can be fun for children. A toddler may be delighted to hand you items you need: your words and expression communicate to him that the book he brought you was just what you wanted. Even young children enjoy your company while laying the table, and they are flattered that you trust them to take responsibility for simple messages. Look at section 2.5 for more ideas.

Stages

You help children learn by your encouragement. Make everyday tasks simpler if necessary and make sure that they can learn in safety. Remember that the process does not have to be all or nothing. Look at it as several stages:

1 *You are totally responsible*
You judge that babies or children cannot manage something or you believe it is not yet safe for them to try, however much they may want to.

2 *You encourage them to join in*
Now you encourage children to help you out a little, though you are still basically in charge. Don't have impossibly high standards or children will be discouraged.

3 *Children take responsibility, but you watch over them*
You say 'Go on, you try it' and you stay close by to help if they need it.

4 *Children are wholly responsible*
You allow children to take responsibility for the task with little or no supervision. Perhaps you check afterwards on what they have done.

Cooking
Children will also start to learn to prepare food and to cook if you can let them learn in safety. Cooking is a most enjoyable activity which can help children in several areas of their development at once:

- they are learning one of the skills of grown-up life;
- they extend their physical skills of co-ordination;
- they learn some basic science, as cooking is a kind of chemistry;
- they also get practice in basic maths, as cooking involves measuring, and calculating times.

Reading on . . .

★ There are a number of books on teaching children to cook. However, if you are a reasonably confident cook you will have plenty of recipes of your own. If you are short of ideas, try *My First Baking Book* (Dorling Kindersley). Jane Asher's *Quick Party Cakes* (Walker Books) has creative plans for amazing-looking cakes from simple ingredients.

★ Our favourite book for teaching children proper cooking is Fay Maschler's *Teach Your Child to Cook* (Bloomsbury). She shows basic techniques which then enable children to branch out into a range of recipes drawn from different cultural traditions.

Dressing
Very young babies cannot help in their physical care; indeed, their waving arms and legs can make apparently simple dressing quite a marathon. Within a few months, however, they are joining in. A baby will push his arms into a sleeve if you hold it out for him. From his point of view, though, this is playtime, so he is just as likely to take his arm out again.

Toddlers who are in the mood may co-operate in dressing. They aim their arms and legs into clothing that you hold out. Most 2- and 3-year-olds learn to manage the simpler parts of dressing. They will learn to pull on hats and slip into or out of loose shoes. They may be able to pull pants or loose trousers down – but probably not back up again. They will find many fastenings difficult and it is not unusual for them to pull hard and hope for the best.

From 3 to 5 years, children learn to tackle the common ways of fastening clothes – buttons, poppers, zips and Velcro. They will have more difficulty if the fastenings are at the back of their clothes or if the garment is tight. Shoelaces are especially difficult and many children escape learning this for some time because of Velcro fastenings on shoes. Look at Chapter 4 to remind yourself that physical skills are needed for these tasks.

You can help by being patient with children as they learn and by doing it for them sometimes. Children benefit from a chance to practise fastenings or shoelaces when there is no pressure of time. You can make or buy a material book that has a button and buttonhole, zip, poppers and a set of laces to tie.

School-age children should be able to dress themselves. They do not, however, all dress or change their clothes at speed. They don't necessarily take good care of their clothes; nor do they always choose clothes of which adults would approve.

Feeding

Babies and young children are usually interested in learning to drink and to feed themselves. Your task is to encourage them in their attempts and gently discourage playing with food or drink. You should be with them throughout meal-times. Never leave a baby or young child alone at a meal-time; she could choke.

Your other task is to tolerate the inevitable mess. Babies and young children will get food and drink over themselves. You need to make sure that it is as easy as possible to clean up children, the surface they eat from and the surrounding floor.

It's possible to overdo the encouraging atmosphere at meal-times

Learning to eat without help

By 6 or 9 months a baby will often put his hand to his bottle or grab the spoon that you are using to feed him. Some younger babies will try this. Soon he may be able to drink, with little help, from a bottle or trainer cup. He may get a little food into his mouth but you will need to feed most of the meal to him with a second spoon. He may also experiment with flicking food or spitting it out again.

In the second half of his first year a baby may also be able to hold onto something firm like a rusk and chew it. He will feed himself if some of his food is suitable for eating with fingers.

From 1 to 2 years of age, young children steadily get better at handling cups with a lid, and getting food into their mouths. They are still not very neat eaters and they may need your help and encouragement to finish off a meal. Gradually 2- and 3-year-olds become more confident and slightly neater in eating and drinking; 3- and 4-year-olds can learn to dish up for themselves or others with a spoon from a serving dish. You still need to accept the inevitable spills and drips. They can also learn to spread food like jam or peanut butter on bread.

By 5 years children will be able largely to feed themselves by whatever method of eating they have learned. This may be chopsticks, fingers, knives and forks, or spoons; or using bread or a similar food as a utensil. Some 6- and 7-year-olds may still need some help in cutting up meat, or in getting meat or poultry off the bone; if most of the cutting up has been done in the cooking process, then children are more likely to be able to serve and feed themselves.

Neat eating and table manners

Your own childhood will have influenced your beliefs about the meaning of eating 'properly' and the importance, or not, of table manners. Take a look at section 2.1 to help you think about this.

You will want to teach children courteous behaviour at meal-times. Do be careful that you don't claim that a rule is universal when in fact it is simply a cultural tradition. However, there may be some basics for children to learn which are more or less universal – don't crowd other eaters, don't sneak other people's food and don't dump your unwanted bits.

Different cultures and different periods of history have varying rules about how to carry on at meal-times. It is important that you are aware of differences as you teach younger children to feed themselves: respect the family's way. However, with older children you can explore various ways of eating. Communicate to them that ways different from their own are only different, not exotic or odd.

Reading on . . .

Some of the books in these series may help you:
★   the 'Our Culture' series, published by Franklin Watts;
★   the 'Phototalk Books' series, from the ILEA Learning Resources Branch.

Toilet-training

Previous generations of parents and workers in the Western world were advised to start toilet-training children from a young age, sometimes even in babyhood. The more usual practice now is to wait until children are at least 18 months and watch for when they seem ready to try the pot or toilet. Nurseries and other centres for children will have low-level toilets, otherwise you will need a special child seat to place on a normal-sized toilet and a safe step for the child to get onto the seat.

If you start too soon, toilet-training will take longer and probably be more frustrating both for you and the child. There is little point in trying unless a child is aware of when he is urinating or passing a bowel movement. It is preferable to wait until he is starting to recognise the physical sensation that comes just before it happens.

Some children develop this awareness within their second year. Some can be fairly well toilet-trained for daytime by 2 years of age. However, this is very variable. Some children really only get the idea of what you want after 2 years of age.

The basics of toilet-training a child who seems ready are these:

●   *Getting used to the idea*   You encourage her to sit for a short while on the pot or toilet several times within the day.

●   *Appropriate encouragement*   If she urinates or passes a bowel movement while on the pot then you tell her 'Well done', but without going on and on about it.

●   *Beginning to wear pants*   When she has only a few wet or soiled nappies within the day, you explain that she can try wearing pants. You need to encourage regular visits to the pot or toilet.

- *Be prepared for accidents*   Be patient and as calm as possible about the inevitable accidents. Be pleased with her every time she uses the pot or toilet successfully.
- *Continued encouragement*   Continue being pleased with her for some months. Don't be surprised if she goes backwards in toilet-training, especially if there is a change in her life such as the arrival of a new baby in the family.

Many 3-year-olds are toilet-trained for the daytime, however you should still expect occasional wet pants, especially if the child is not able to get to a toilet swiftly. Children may also wet themselves if they have a long nap. They have only a limited ability to hold on; you can help by reminding them to go to the toilet at regular intervals in their nursery or playgroup. When you go out together, it is your task to find the toilets quickly.

Children with physical disabilities may have more difficulty in achieving control, or it may never be within their grasp. Much will depend on the nature of their disability.

Many 4-year-olds are becoming dry during the night-time as well – this is also very variable. Some children do not manage this if they are left for the whole of their sleeping time. Some 4- and 5-year-olds are lifted up and carried to go to the toilet when their parents go to bed.

Most school-age children have full control of their bladder and bowels by day and night. However, some children will not have managed, although there is no obvious physical problem. The children will be increasingly upset and embarrassed over their failure in control. The Enuresis Resource and Information Centre (ERIC; address below) estimates that bed-wetting, at least, affects over half a million children between 6 and 16 years old in Britain.

TO THINK ABOUT

1   Remember children whom you have toilet-trained. How much variety have you experienced in the age at which they were reliably dry and clean in the daytime?

Compare experiences with your colleagues.

2   Are you caring for children over 3 years of age who still have many toileting accidents not explained by physical disability?

Can you see practical ways to help these children? For example, do they have difficulty with tight clothing or hard fastenings? Do they get absorbed in play and need to be encouraged to go to the toilet?

For your information

★   Enuresis Resource and Information Centre (ERIC): 65 St Michael's Hill, Bristol BS2 8DZ (*tel.* 0272 264920). ERIC is a national centre offering information and advice to parents and professionals on the problem of bed-wetting.

Personal care

Even 3- and 4-year-olds can be encouraged to learn basic hygiene for their own care. You can give simple explanations for what you are asking them to do. Basic hygiene could include the following.

Cleanliness

Children should wash their hands after going to the toilet and before eating or helping with food. In a group, young children can learn to use only their own flannel or towel.

Hair care

Even toddlers enjoy brushing their hair with a simple brush or comb. Getting knots out of long or curly hair is a more difficult task. You will need a wide-toothed comb for black children to use.

Teeth

If you work on a daytime basis with children you might only be talking about care of teeth. Not all dentists recommend brushing teeth after each meal: some are concerned that over-brushing can damage tooth enamel.

Skin care

You may need to use cream on a child if her skin becomes dry and cracked. This is a normal part of daily care for many dark-skinned children and should be discussed with the child's parents. You may not need to put cream on the child unless she has a long day with you or perhaps if you take her swimming. Some 4- and 5-year-olds may like to help with the creaming.

If a child in your care has eczema, she will need some prescribed cream. Talk over with her parents what they would like you to do. If the child needs the stronger creams then you should do all the creaming, although she will need to learn to take care of her needs when she is older.

All children need protection against the sun when they are playing outside in hot weather. Pale-skinned children will be the first to burn but dark-skinned children will also get sunburn and heatstroke if you're not careful. Discuss with parents any plans to use sun-protection creams on their children and ask them to send in a sun hat that their child is willing to wear. In a long hot spell you will have to ration all children's time in direct sun and make sure that they drink plenty.

TO THINK ABOUT

If you are under a lot of pressure – perhaps because your centre is short-staffed – then you may very much want children to feed and dress themselves without much help from you, but this may be asking too much of 3- and 4-year-olds, let alone 2-year-olds.

1 Within the last few weeks, what have you expected the children to manage largely without help from you?

- Going to the toilet?
- Putting on hats and coats to go outside?
- Eating a meal?   ▶ *continued*

2   Looking back over section 3.3, do you think you expect too much? Or do you have realistic expectations, but forget to compliment children on their ability to feed or dress themselves?

Sometimes young children appear uncooperative and demand your help. It may be their way of asking for some personal attention.

TO THINK ABOUT

Everyday skills may seem ordinary but this doesn't mean they're easy skills to learn. You learned physical skills like tying shoelaces or cutting up your food a long time ago. Do you recall how difficult these tasks used to seem?

For example, suppose that a 3-year-old is learning to pour herself a drink from a jug. She has to look carefully at the jug, pick it up, and hold it steady as she moves it to her cup. She has to concentrate on holding the jug and looking at the cup as she starts to pour. She has to stop before the drink goes over the top of her cup. Then she has to straighten the jug and look carefully as she moves it back and places it down on the table.

1   Look carefully at all that is involved in some other very ordinary activities that young children are learning. List the separate steps that children have to go through. You could think about any of the following.

- cutting up a piece of meat or chicken;
- turning an inside-out sweatshirt around the right way;
- buttoning up a shirt or blouse;
- doing up an open-ended zip on a coat;
- tying shoelaces.

2   Does the list of steps help you to see how you can help children in learning these tasks?

3.4 Infections and special health needs

In this section we give brief information on some illnesses and medical conditions. Our aim is to give enough detail to help you seek out more advice when you need it.

We have *not* attempted to tell you how to diagnose illness or exactly how to nurse children who are ill. Nor have we attempted to give detailed advice on working with children with disabilities.

When children fall ill

You are trying to keep children as healthy as possible. However, every child will be ill at some point during childhood. Some will suffer from more ill-health than others.

When a child in your care seems to be ill, you have the difficult task of deciding:

- What is the matter?
- How serious is it? And therefore . . .
- Do you need to contact the child's parent?

Babies and young children cannot say much to guide you when they are ill or sickening for something. You can check temperature and any signs of rashes or swellings, and there may be more obvious events such as vomiting or diarrhoea. However, you have to rely a great deal on observing changes from their usual behaviour.

When you are sharing the care of babies with their parents it is especially important that you talk together when one hands over responsibility to the other. If a baby or child is poorly you both need to have accurate information on how long this has lasted. Vomiting and diarrhoea can be especially dangerous for babies.

Most 4- and 5-year-olds will be better able to tell you what is wrong. Children, however, like adults, are going to be subjective in answering 'How much does it hurt?', and some may still be confused about names for parts of the body. You need to ask 'Show me' as well as 'Tell me'.

Books on children's health give the likely signs of common childhood diseases like mumps or chicken pox. What you look for will differ slightly, of course, depending on children's skin colour.

If children are pale-skinned, then spots or an unusual flush will show up as red against their skin. Pale-skinned children with high temperatures may look unnaturally flushed or may be drained of their usual rosy cheeks.

The darker a child's skin colour, the more spots or a rash will show simply as raised areas. You may notice a different shading of skin colour around the spots. As soon as children start scratching, the spots will show as more red and any blistering will be noticeable. Dark-skinned children may drain of colour, too, in contrast with how they look usually.

Reading on . . .

★ Carter, Margaret 1989: *You and Your Child in Hospital* (Methuen).
★ Lansdown, Richard 1980: *More than Sympathy – the everyday needs of sick and handicapped children* (Tavistock).

★ Smith, Mike 1992: *Handbook of Over-the-Counter Medicines* (Kyle Cathie).
★ Smith, Tony 1992: *The Macmillan Guide to Family Health* (Macmillan).
★ VOLCUF 1991: *Keeping Children Healthy – a guide for under-fives workers*.

Children's feelings and illness

Babies and children who are ill can feel anything from mildly under the weather through to really sick. Depending on the illness these feelings will pass. Some children, however, have a continuing condition that affects their overall level of health; they need extra emotional support, because they may begin to view themselves largely in terms of their physical ill-health or disability. Children may feel embarrassed about symptoms or their inability to play like other children.

How to help

You can be helpful in the following ways, all of which should be in partnership with the child's parents.

Find out about the condition
Discuss with her parents how you can all help the child to understand any debilitating condition from which she suffers. Obviously this depends on the age of the child. Be ready for the time when she could start to learn some of the care that she needs – for example, using an inhaler if she has asthma.

Affirm the child as a person
Talk and play with the child with the aim of helping her to see herself as separate from the illness. Ideally she should be able to say and think, for instance, 'I am Rachel and I have diabetes', not 'I am a diabetic'.

What might you need to do?
Make sure that you know, by discussion with her parents, what you should be doing for this child in daily care and if she becomes suddenly ill – for example, what to do for a child who has sickle-cell anaemia and who develops a fever. The child's experience will be worse if she senses that you are in a panic.

What do the other children need to know?
You may need to explain simply to other children what this child has to bear. Discuss what you will say with her parents and if possible with the child as well. For example, even mild eczema can be a source of embarrassment to children: they may resist undressing for games or swimming, and they expect other children to tease them or to move away, claiming that the condition is catching.

Be tactful but straightforward
Don't criticise children for asking questions or for noticing differences. Answer their questions honestly and simply. Encourage them to be tactful in how and when they ask such questions, and to address their queries to the child or adult concerned. You will need to deal with some unrealistic beliefs that some conditions are catching when they are not.

The child may be absent for some time
If an illness causes a child to be absent for long periods, be ready to help her re-establish friendships and remember nursery or playgroup routine. A child in the early years of school may need help with study as well.

Children with disabilities

Similar considerations are equally important if you are caring for a child with disabilities. Children can be cruel in their remarks to those who have a disability, but this is not inevitable. You can help by chatting with children when any child is going to join an existing group, but this can be especially important if that child is likely to be viewed as different in some way.

For example, you can take a positive approach to introducing Malcolm who is in a wheelchair. Before Malcolm arrives, prepare the other children to notice what Malcolm can do as much as what he cannot. Fully able children may also want to be reassured that Malcolm is not going to be allowed to get away with breaking group rules just because he has a disability. Do not, of course, talk about Malcolm in front of him as if he were not present.

Using books and other resources

You need to use material in two equally important ways.

First, there are books and programmes on television that are informative about different illnesses and conditions. These should provide information that is useful for all children.

Secondly, these sources of information should help you establish that children who have persistent illness or disability are first and foremost *children*. You confirm this message for all children by buying or borrowing stories that feature children who *happen* to be in wheelchairs or be troubled with asthma, but who in the story are getting on with their lives and playing with their friends.

Reading on . . .

There are good books that will help you. Ask your local library or a bookshop to search if necessary. These are examples:
★ Some of Nigel Snell's books in the 'Events' series, published by Hamish Hamilton.
★ The 'One World' series, published by Franklin Watts. Starting with the words 'I have . . .', different books in the series cover many conditions and illnesses.
★ Helen Young's *What Difference Does it Make Danny?* published by Fontana Young Lions. A story to read in episodes for the older children or for you to read to gain insight into epilepsy.
★ Emily Hearn's stories about Franny, who is in a wheelchair – *Franny and the Music Girl*, *Race You Franny*, and others. Some books are published by Magi and some by the Women's Press.
★ Micheline Watson's *Nothing Special*, published by the Working Press (85 St Agnes Place, London SE11 4BB).
★ Sue Brearley's *Adventure Holiday*, published by A & C Black.

Non-infectious conditions

Some children have a debilitating condition that affects their overall level of health, leading them to feel ill most of the time or giving them bouts of illness. However, they cannot infect other children.

Eczema

Eczema is a miserable problem for a child to have, even in a mild version. Children can get very irritated by itchy skin, and will be in pain if their skin cracks and bleeds. Most children seem to outgrow the condition, at least to an extent, however about 10 per cent will continue to suffer throughout their lives. A child's parents and her doctor will need to decide on treatment and to review its effectiveness regularly.

You should follow the pattern established by the family. You may not have to put cream on children unless they have a long day with you and their condition is bad. You need to avoid anything that parents explain worsens the condition: this may mean using some particular soap or making sure that the child avoids some foods. Some children need to avoid any contact with certain materials which might be in the dressing-up box.

Asthma

Asthma is the most common chronic medical disorder of childhood: about 10 per cent of children suffer from it. Some have only mild attacks but about half of sufferers have more serious attacks with bad coughing fits and breathing problems. A minority have persistent problems, with attacks most days.

In discussion with a child's parents you need to find out the following.

- *What are the signs that this child is likely to have an attack and what should you do?* He may have an inhaler which you will have to help him use. You may be able to help most by calm behaviour and by helping him to sit in the best position to breathe.

- *Should you avoid giving the child certain foods?* His parents may have found that eggs or chocolate, for instance, can bring on an attack.

- *Are there any danger signs that mean you should get the child to hospital?*

Hay fever

This term covers allergies to different tree and plant pollens and other substances such as house dust. The symptoms are like those of a heavy cold – runny nose, sneezing and coughing. Sufferers can get itchy eyes which become red and swollen. There are now some medications that counteract the symptoms without causing drowsiness.

Hay fever seems to run in families. It is often linked with asthma or other allergies.

Reading on . . .
Here are two books that could help you:
★   Carson, Paul 1987: *How to Cope with your Child's Allergies* (Sheldon Press).

★   Steel, Mary 1986: *Understanding Allergies* (The Consumers' Association).

Sickle-cell disease

Sickle-cell disease is an inherited blood disorder. Though more common in families who originated from Africa or the Caribbean, it also occurs in families from the Eastern Mediterranean, the Middle East, India and Pakistan. The most common and severe form is sickle-cell anaemia. This is different from the anaemia that people can develop as a result of iron deficiency.

About 1 in every 400 Afro-Caribbean people in Britain has sickle-cell anaemia. They are not necessarily ill all the time, but both children and adults may suffer from crises. These are episodes of severe anaemia and pain, which need urgent hospital treatment. Talk with parents to understand the signs of a crisis for their child.

Children with sickle-cell are more vulnerable to minor infections and fevers: you should tell their parents about any infection sweeping through a group. Children need extra care to keep them warm and should probably avoid playing out in cold and damp weather. They need to drink plenty — dehydration or vigorous exercise may trigger a crisis.

Thalassaemia

Thalassaemia is another inherited blood disorder. It is most common in Mediterranean countries such as Greece, Turkey, Cyprus and Italy, but it also occurs in the Middle East. Adults and children with thalassaemia need regular blood transfusions. This can lead to an excess of iron in the body, which has to be corrected by injections. With appropriate medical treatment, children can enjoy an otherwise normal childhood.

Epilepsy and fits

Epilepsy results from a problem in the brain's communication system. The tiny electrical signals from one group of nerve cells become stronger than normal and overwhelm nearby parts of the brain. This sudden, excessive electrical discharge is what brings on an epileptic fit. Not all fits are caused by epilepsy: some young children have brief fits brought on by fever and high temperature.

Parents should tell you if their child has fits and how you should handle these. You need to know if there is any pattern to a child's fits, including how long they usually last. What follows is only very general advice.

Epileptic fits can be major or minor. Minor fits (petit mal) tend to be a problem of childhood and often do not outlast late adolescence. Children suffering a petit mal seizure may go blank for seconds or up to a minute or so. The child may jerk her head or limbs slightly. In a major seizure (grand mal) a child is likely to fall to the ground and her body will stiffen and then jerk uncontrollably. This may last for a few minutes and she may lose bladder or bowel control.

* *Stay with the child*   You will help best by staying by the child and making sure that she emerges from the fit.

* *Wait with her and protect her*   Stay calm. Don't try to force her out of it and don't move her unless she is in danger, for example if she is in the middle of the road. If she is having a major fit, make sure that she cannot

hurt herself or others. Move objects out of her way or cover them with a padding like a blanket. *Don't* put your fingers in her mouth or try to force anything between her jaws.

- *Recovery* When she has emerged from the fit, put her in the recovery position (see any first aid book, or the VOLCUF booklet given earlier in this section) and let her rest. Keep her comfortable and watch over her. Call her parents. Call for medical help if she does not awake after about 15 minutes.

- *Long or recurring fits* Most fits only last a minute or two. If a fit lasts more than about three minutes, or if a child starts another fit a few minutes after the first, then call for emergency medical help.

For your information

Addresses for information and advice on some debilitating conditions:

- British Epilepsy Association: Anstey House, 40 Hanover Square, Leeds L53 1BE (*tel.* general 0532 439393; advice 0345 089599).
- National Asthma Campaign: 300 Upper Street, London N1 2XX (*tel.* 071–226 2260).
- National Eczema Society: Tavistock House North, Tavistock Square, London WC1H 9SR (*tel.* 071–388 4097).
- Sickle Cell Society: 54 Station Road, Harlesden, London NW10 4BU (*tel.* 081–961 7795).
- United Kingdom Thalassaemia Society: 107 Nightingale Lane, London N8 7QY (*tel.* 081–348 0437).

AIDS and HIV

AIDS (Acquired Immune Deficiency Syndrome) is a condition in which the immune system is seriously weakened. It appears to be caused by a virus named the Human Immunodeficiency Virus (HIV). The nature of the condition and exactly how it is caused is still not fully understood. You will need to update yourself.

The condition can be passed on but nothing like as easily as some media scares have implied. People can be infected with the virus and yet remain apparently healthy for years. When AIDS develops, normally minor illness and infections can make individuals very ill indeed. Children and adults then have bouts of ill-health with temporary remissions. At the time of writing, in 1992, AIDS is a fatal condition, although there is some progress in delaying the disease's pattern.

The HIV virus lives in the body fluids of an individual, and is passed on only through very intimate contact. Adults have been infected through sexual contact, re-use of hypodermic needles, and receiving infected blood in transfusions. Babies and children have been infected through the placenta before birth; there is also concern that the virus could pass through breast milk. Some children with haemophilia were infected by blood transfusions before the risk was recognised.

Current medical advice is that children with HIV or AIDS cannot infect workers or other children through playing or the normal contact between friends. Follow the standards for hygiene described in section 3.1 for dealing with all children.

Reading on . . .

★ National Children's Bureau: *Aids and Children* ('Highlight' No. 95).
★ Griffiths, Ronno (ed.): *HIV/AIDS and the Under-Fives – a guide for workers and carers*, from the Manchester AIDSline Women's Group, PO Box 201, Manchester M60 1PU.

Lice and worms

Most children will experience at least one visitation from these common parasites. The children will not be ill but may be in a lot of discomfort and will be tired if their sleep is disturbed.

If you work on a daily basis with children and their families, you are unlikely to be treating children for the condition. You will need to inform parents if you discover signs of lice or worms. This will not be the most enjoyable conversation of your working life, especially if it is the parents' first encounter with the problem! Make the conversation private and make it practical.

It is a good idea to give some general information to all parents at a time when their own child is not infected. You will often find leaflets in child clinics or on the counter at the chemist's.

The basics you need to remember are as follows.

Head lice

The first sign is likely to be that a child keeps scratching part of her head. You may see the lice themselves but they are small. Alternatively you may see their eggs, called nits; these are small white specks which look rather like dandruff.

Special anti-lice shampoos are available over the counter from chemists – ordinary shampoos will not kill lice. The eggs need to be removed by combing the child's hair with a special fine-toothed nit comb. Some parents react with horror to the first experience of head lice and insist on cutting their children's hair very short. This is absolutely unnecessary and will probably distress children.

The best preventive action against head lice is to make sure that children's hair is thoroughly combed morning and evening. This clears the hair of eggs and dead lice and breaks the legs of any live ones – their days will then be numbered.

Threadworms

These are tiny white worms which can get onto children's hands from contaminated food, or just as easily from toilets or even the earth. Children put their hands to their mouths and the eggs enter their body. These eggs hatch in the child's intestine and about two weeks later the female threadworm lays eggs around the child's anus, usually at night. This causes a most uncomfortable itching.

You can buy a mixture from the chemists to flush out threadworms: it works by giving children mild diarrhoea. Children are in agreement that it tastes pretty bad. There may still be a night or two when children are hard pressed to resist scratching. It helps if you cut their fingernails and have the children in pyjamas or a pair of close-fitting pants so that they cannot make themselves sore with scratching.

You might need to reassure parents that it is not necessary to make a bonfire of their possessions! Thorough washing of combs and brushes and of bedding is usually enough.

There are simple practical steps you can take against threadworms:

- *Handwashing* Teach children to wash their hands before meal-times or cooking activities, and always after going to the toilet.
- *General hygiene* Make sure that toilets and washbasins are clean and disinfected. They should not be allowed to run out of soap or toilet paper. Children should not share towels or flannels.

3.5 Helping children in distress

We are looking at two different sets of experiences in this section. Firstly we look at how you can help children with distressing events that are within the normal ups and downs of life for many children. Then we look separately at the experience of abuse, which is part of life for some children.

Upsetting experiences

All children will have some unhappy experiences in their childhood. They may be upset by a bad tumble or the harsh word of a friend. Sometimes children are frightened or confused by something they see on television, or by a misunderstood scrap of conversation overheard from adults.

They may be worried by an event that is new or unknown, such as going into hospital or the unexpected changes brought about by the arrival of a new baby. Some children are distressed by serious upheavals such as the death of a close relative or the break-up of their family.

Some adults persist in believing that even very distressing events go over children's heads; they avoid talking with children about the experiences, hoping perhaps that children will forget. However, children need to express their feelings to someone whom they trust and who cares about them. Often this will be through play and conversation at home with their parents, but often it will be with you.

You can help children by the following:

- *Affirm them*   Listen to what children tell you and show that you believe their feelings matter.

- *Respond to them*   Be alert to them in their play and be ready to ask gently, 'Is anything the matter?'

- *Listen to them*   Lend a sympathetic ear to a child who wishes to tell you her troubles. Give her the same respect of confidentiality that you would to an adult.

- *Talk with them*   Talk over with an older child what she might be able to do in facing a particular difficulty.

- *Be ready to help them*   If those troubles are with another child in your group, then you may decide you should step in to help. Chapter 7 offers ideas about dealing with children's behaviour.

- *Consider talking with their parents*   If the problem is outside your group, you will almost certainly need to talk with her parents. Even if the difficulty seems minor, your conversation will be easier if you have developed a good working relationship with her parents. (Section 2.4 covers partnership with parents.)

Children can learn by weathering upsetting experiences and learning ways of coping where possible. You can help by showing them that you take their feelings seriously. Look at Chapter 6 to remind yourself of children's level of ability to understand what is happening.

You can get books that tackle difficult events in the lives of children. These include major events such as death and divorce, and more common-place ones such as going into hospital or seeing the dentist.

For your information

The following series each offer a range of books covering different topics:
★ 'Let's Talk About' (Franklin Watts).
★ 'Facing Up' (Happy Books).
★ 'First Experience' (Usborne).
★ 'Events' (Hamish Hamilton).

Child abuse

Some children have seriously distressing experiences, perhaps inflicted by people they have trusted. Abuse of children is not only carried out by adults – some children are harmed by older children. Section 3.3 has suggestions for helping children protect themselves and feel more confident in seeking help from a trusted adult.

The main kinds of abuse are as follows.

Physical abuse

Someone deliberately injures a child, for example by hitting, burning or attempting to suffocate the child. It would also be classified as physical abuse if a child were given alcohol or inappropriate drugs.

Sexual abuse

Adults or teenagers use children to satisfy their own sexual needs. Abuse is not limited to full sexual intercourse: it would also be sexual abuse of children to fondle their private parts, or to have or attempt to have oral or anal sex. Another form of sexual abuse is to show or involve children in pornography.

Emotional abuse

Emotional abuse could be a daily pattern of being shouted at, threatened or taunted. Children's development can be damaged by continuous coldness or rejection from a parent, even when they are not physically harmed.

Neglect

Children are being neglected when their basic needs for food, clothing and shelter are not met. Some parents may be unable to meet these needs because of dire money troubles or housing problems. You may be able to help by putting parents in touch with organisations or individuals who can help them.

Adults are also neglectful if they leave babies and young children alone or unsupervised in unsafe conditions.

Signs of abuse

The following are possible signs of abuse of children. You should not take *any* of these as proof of abuse *on their own*.

What you see is a pattern of behaviour, and you need to make sense of events for which there may be more than one possible explanation. Discuss your concerns with fellow workers or your senior. Prepare how you will discuss your worries with parents. However, don't delay over this.

Children's behaviour
• *A child's behaviour has changed noticeably* Perhaps a previously

outgoing child has become extremely quiet; or a child has regressed in his development but there is no usual explanation such as the arrival of a new baby.

- *A child plays or makes physical contact with other children or adults in a sexually explicit manner* For example, she tries to fondle other children, or her conversation shows a high awareness of adult sexuality.
- *A child is extremely wary of adults in general or never seems happy to go with a particular person.*
- *A child has many fears and worries* Perhaps you realise from his conversation that he has many nightmares.
- *A child seems to feel worthless, even perhaps hurts himself physically.*

Physical signs

- *A child appears to be receiving very poor care* For instance, he is generally unwell, or losing weight, without any obvious explanation. Or he is regularly smelly or dirty, or extremely hungry, or dressed in clothes that are inappropriate for the weather.
- *A child has bruising around the genital or anal area, which is not explained by a fall or similar accident.*
- *A child has bruises, cuts or burn marks which are not satisfactorily explained by a parent.*

You should be aware that black and mixed-race children often have natural differences in colorations in their skin that can look like bad bruising: these are called Mongolian blue spots. They are often found on the lower spine but may be elsewhere on the body. They do not need any treatment and often fade as the child grows.

What should you do?

Working closely with children who have been abused or with their families is a specialist task, needing further training. However, the following is relevant to all workers.

Be observant
Observe children who are your responsibility and check out any behaviour or physical signs that make you uneasy.

Know what is normal among children
Remember the normal range of children's behaviour. For example, most children are curious about bodies and have a giggling fascination with going to the toilet.

Know what is normal in different families
If you do not have children of your own, then try to be aware of the nature of normal family life and the differences of culture and tradition.

For example, many young children attempt to slip into their parents' bed on occasion. Some families have strict views about modesty; in others parents have a bath or shower with their young children. The majority of parents can enjoy close physical contact with their children and *not* wish in any way to abuse the children.

Listen to what children say

Young children may reveal an experience of abuse to you through words or their play. If children want to talk with you, then follow their lead.

- *Show respect*   Show that you take what they say seriously; that you are not brushing their words or feelings aside. (A careful investigation will later have to be made to determine the truth of a child's claims.)

- *Don't lead*   Avoid pointed questions like 'Was it Uncle who did this to you?'

- *Give open responses*   If the child is looking to you to say something, you can ask open-ended questions like 'What happened?' and 'How did you feel about that?' Or you can simply repeat some part of what the child has said in a gently questioning tone of voice.

- *Let the child set the pace*   Stop the conversation as soon as the child wishes. You should not interview the child in any structured way, unless you have been trained in this.

Don't promise the child to keep quiet about what you've been told

You can explain with words like, 'I can keep happy secrets but if you have an unhappy secret, I will have to tell someone else so that we can help you.'

Take advice

If you are working in a nursery, school or hospital, you should report to your senior what has happened. You or your senior will have to talk informally with the child's parent very soon.

Don't contact anyone official until you have checked whether there is an explanation that seems credible. However, if you remain concerned then you or your senior should contact the local social services or the NSPCC. No nursery, school or playgroup should undertake formal investigations before sharing their concerns with other agencies.

Keep notes

Write up what has happened as soon as possible, preferably within the same day. You should follow a pattern such as:

- *What happened?*   Make notes of what you saw, for example bruises or a burn mark. Record any explanation given to you by parents. If you are describing a pattern of behaviour from a child, give details of what the child does and when you observed this. If a child has told you about abuse, note down afterwards the child's words as accurately as you can. Also note down what you said in return.

- *Why are you worried?*   This is more subjective and might include any doubts you have about the explanation given by a parent for a mark. It might also include your overall impressions from a conversation with a child.

Seek support for yourself

Dealing with child abuse or the suspicion of abuse is an emotionally stressful experience. You need and deserve support, including a chance to express *your* feelings in confidence.

Reading on . . .

★   Kids Club Network 1990: *The Role of Playcare Workers in the Protection of Children from Abuse.*
★   Rouf, Khadj and Anne Peake 1990: *Working with Sexually Abused Children – a resource pack for professionals.* Available from the Children's Society, Edward Rudolf House, Margery Street, London WC1X OJL (*tel.* 071–837 4299).
★   VOLCUF 1990: *Child Abuse – a guide for under-fives workers.*

4 Physical development

4.1 Children's physical development 0–7

Similarities and variations

Children's physical abilities develop as they grow older. In this section we describe some general patterns and give the approximate ages of children at which you may expect to see these. However, you will notice variation between babies or children of a given age.

What children do and how well they do it depends on personal qualities such as their level of confidence or recklessness. It also depends on what is available for them to do, and what adults allow or encourage them to try.

For example, under-2s can use their improved level of coordination to paint. If the adults around them find the inevitable mess hard to tolerate, however, then the children may be denied this opportunity until they are older.

Babies and children share common patterns in learning physical skills. Don't expect all children to follow exactly the same order, though. Many babies learn to crawl before they walk, for example, whereas some babies shuffle along on their bottoms instead of crawling. Other babies take a few teetering steps and then drop to all fours to crawl for weeks before trying to walk again.

From birth to 3 months

Muscle control

Babies are born with a set of innate reflex movements such as sucking; they have a surprisingly strong grip, evident if you place your finger in their palm. Premature babies may not have such strong reactions and some of these reflexes fade in all babies within a few days of birth.

Proportionately, babies' heads are rather heavy and large for the rest of their body. Newborns don't have the muscle control to hold up their head even for a moment. Over the weeks they gain control, starting from the head and then moving down through the body. By 6 weeks or so, babies in your arms may hold their head steady for a little while.

In the early weeks, babies' physical movements look jerky and their arms tend to be more active than their legs. However, with your supporting hold, for example in the bathwater, they can kick or push quite strongly.

Babies take a while to uncurl

Interest and looking

Babies of a few weeks old spread and flex their fingers and sometimes stare

at them in a rather perplexed manner. They gaze intently at an adult's face when they are cuddled or fed. Very young babies are best able to focus at the distance between their face and that of an adult holding them. After a couple of months, babies become able to follow with their eyes something of interest that is moving, like a mobile.

Around 3 months of age

Movements

By 3 months of age, babies have gained control of their head and shoulders. They will be beginning to be able to move themselves by rolling from lying on their back to their side. They no longer stay in the position in which you laid them down.

They begin to make stronger and more purposeful movements with their arms and hands. Often, though, they cannot get hold of an interesting object and so depend on you to put it into their hands so that they can explore it by feeling and looking.

Curiosity

Young babies show a curiosity about their surroundings, some quite early on. Certainly by 3 months they should be taking an interest in what goes on around them. They look hard and, within their physical abilities, will turn towards sounds or glimpses.

From 3 to 6 months

Gaining physical control

Within these months, babies' muscle control moves downwards until they can hold up their head, shoulders and then their back. By 6 months they may be able to sit for a very short while, but they fall off balance.

Playing

Babies become fascinated by the greater control they can now exert over their own hands and fingers, and they happily play with their fingers and toes.

Soon they may manage to hold a rattle for a short while. They will learn to shake the rattle but are quite likely to hit themselves by mistake. They will reach out to grasp anything that interests them. They use their whole hand to grasp and may manage to pass a toy from one hand to another.

At 3 or 4 months old, babies benefit from playtime on the floor. They need to lie on a soft surface like a rug or blanket, free from draughts. If there are rushing older children or curious pets nearby, they may need to be in a playpen, but they shouldn't spend a lot of their time in this.

By 6 months, babies will most likely be able to shift their weight in order to roll from one position to another. Applying their ability on the floor will allow them to reach parts of a room that were previously, and safely, out of reach.

From 6 to 12 months

Sitting and moving

From 6 to 9 months babies are learning to sit without support. They get better at turning to watch events and reaching out for objects. Initially, too ambitious a lean to one side will topple them over. They are learning to move themselves around at surprising speed – using skills of crawling, rolling or bottom-shuffling.

Towards 10–12 months babies start to pull themselves up by holding onto furniture or anything else that has the height they want. They make no judgement about whether their handhold is secure: *you* have to ensure that the room is safe for them.

Physical play

Babies enjoy making noises by shaking, bashing or dropping objects. They will use anything that comes to hand. They explore any object by taking it to their mouth.

By 9 months, babies are exploring objects in other ways as well. You will see them turning objects over and poking them. They feel soft toys and like to scrunch up or rip paper. They like dropping toys or food over the edge of a highchair and watch with interest as these land.

You can teach them to discriminate between food – which you don't want flung – and toys, which *can* be dropped. You will find it hard not to laugh at some of the antics and babies will often repeat an action that amused you.

Babies hold up their arms, asking to be picked up. Most of them love being bounced up and down with their legs braced against your lap or a firm surface.

By the end of the first year, babies have favourite toys. In their play, they like to make piles of objects. They enjoy tipping things out of containers and they try to put simple objects together. By 12 months they have a range of basic physical skills for exploring what can be done even with small objects. They continue to learn by exploration, and by watching and copying what adults and other children do.

If a baby is affected by some disability, the pattern of physical development may be different; and a very premature baby may not achieve these physical skills until an older age.

He loves *playing with his toes*

ACTIVITY

1   Observe the mobility of two babies who are coming up for their first birthday.

- How does each baby move around – crawling? bottom-shuffling? walking?
- How quickly can they move from one side of a medium-sized room to another? (Obviously, you should make sure that they cannot get into trouble whilst you are timing them.)

2   Talk with their parents.

- What modifications have they had to make to their home in order to keep their mobile baby safe? (Or what changes had they already made for an older sibling?)

From 1 to 2 years

Moving around

At 1 year old children will be moving about by crawling, bottom-shuffling or using furniture as handholds. They may be walking by now; if not, they will be within the next few months.

They are becoming more able to adjust their position – for example, they may move confidently from sitting to standing. They look steadier when they are reaching out for something. They learn to move from a standing position to squatting down and then straighten up again.

Within this year, toddlers walk, climb and begin to run – with no idea of danger whatsoever. Inevitably, they have tumbles and collisions with people and furniture. They focus on what they want and where they want to go and their turn of speed often outstrips their ability to swerve and stop.

An 18-month-old can combine several physical skills in a sequence. You may admire their ingenuity but you will worry about the consequences. For example, children of this age may drag a chair across the room so that they can climb up onto it to reach into a cupboard.

By 18 months old toddlers can often climb up stairs, perhaps with a helping hand. They probably come downstairs by creeping backwards. It is safer to teach them to climb stairs than to try to keep them away.

Varied play

Toddlers enjoy more play materials now that they can call on a wider range of physical skills.

They push around wheeled carts, enjoying loading and unloading them. They learn to propel themselves on push-along bikes – often at some speed.

The under-2s become increasingly adept at finding, picking up and using all kinds of objects, large and small. They may build simple brick towers and laugh as they then knock them down. By 18 months they can probably pick up even little objects with a finger-and-thumb grasp. They may examine these objects, and unfortunately they may then put them into their mouth or up their nose.

Young children do not distinguish between toys and all other objects: *anything* interesting is worth their attention. The advantage of this is that safe household objects, like wooden spoons, can be a source of happy play. The disadvantage is that they will be as interested in a cup of hot coffee as in a toy cup. You have to be constantly vigilant.

Given the opportunity, toddlers will enjoy simple painting and drawing. By 15 months, many can make marks with a fat crayon or wield a thick paint brush. Their creative activity is naturally likely to be very messy.

They can enjoy picture books and are not bothered by the fact that they turn several pages at a time. You can teach them not to rip the pages or suck them. By 2 years old, their pleasure in looking at books and magazines grows as they recognise familiar objects and spot even small details in picture books.

All of this is possible by the time children reach their second birthday. The change in two years is stunning. The new baby who used to cry to be fed now runs off to raid the biscuit tin before she is caught. Of course, children with disabilities will need additional help and encouragement to persist, and some changes to their immediate environment may be necessary to make movement possible or safe for them.

TO THINK ABOUT

The world is a very different place to a sighted child and to a partially sighted child who has to depend on the feel of objects.

A very mobile toddler will be annoyed when she is removed from interesting cupboards or what she sees as playthings. A child who has a disability limiting control of her limbs may become very frustrated in her attempts to move and reach for things.

Try to see the world of a child with disabilities. You may find it hard to imagine what this is like.

From 2 to 4 years

Physical abilities

Children grow in physical confidence so long as they are given the opportunity to practise what they can do in safe surroundings.

Children are learning some sense of danger within this age range, but it is far from complete. They do not put everything in their mouths as babies do; but they still suck objects, even if absent-mindedly. Their playthings no longer have to be sterile but they should be safe and clean.

They will develop in all the following skills.

Running

Between 2 and 3, children develop both speed and skill in running. They may still crash into things, but probably less often now.

Climbing

With the opportunity to practise, 2-year-olds will manage stairs, although they may still come down two feet to a step. Even older children can still be in danger of falling if they rush.

Some 3- and 4-year-olds may be skilled climbers but are unlikely to restrict using their skill to what *you* view as appropriate climbing equipment.

Jumping

Many 2-year-olds often become interested in jumping games provided that you hold their hand; 3-year-olds will jump from low heights, like steps. You can teach them to bend their knees as they land. On a firm surface they learn to jump with two feet together – they find this difficult at first.

Playing with games equipment

At some point girls and boys will try to roll or kick a ball. They will almost certainly find it very hard to catch a ball, even a big one.

Balance and movement

Some 3-year-olds are able to work the pedals of a tricycle; some 4-year-olds can manage a bicycle with trainer wheels.

Some 4-year-olds have a good enough sense of balance to enjoy walking along a line. Some can walk along low-level gymnastic equipment. They may enjoy learning the difficult movements of running on tiptoe or hopping.

Many 3- and 4-year-olds love moving to music as well as energetic dancing.

Building and creative activities

Most 2-, 3- and 4-year-olds enjoy making things. Their physical control now enables them to learn skills like using small- and larger-scale construction material. They are able to persevere in learning the ability to cut and stick. Because they are gaining a finer control of crayons and paint brushes, they are able to produce an ever wider selection of artwork.

By 2 and 3 three years old they can enjoy jigsaws. They apply their skills of looking and picking up and handling small objects. They also need to learn an experimental approach to fitting things together. Some children enjoy this challenge more than others.

Section 4.2 gives suggestions for play activities with children.

TO THINK ABOUT

1 You need to consider how you help young children, as they do not always want you to step in and complete something for them.

Even 3- and 4-year-olds' ability to pick up and fit objects together does not always match their more grandiose plans. You need to give children discreet help and plenty of praise for their end-product.

2 You show that you are serious in your praise when you find a place to display children's work. Remember that many homes do not have a lot of space.

If parents groan at yet another huge painting or eggbox rocket, it doesn't necessarily mean that they are unappreciative of the children's efforts!

7-year-olds have impressive physical skills

The over-5s

Physical skills

From 5 to 7 years, children get faster, stronger and more confident of their physical skills. They enjoy games using a wide range of equipment – balls and bats, a skipping rope, hoops, and all kinds of climbing and riding equipment.

Of course, not every individual child is equally adept at a given physical skill, but all children will improve with practice. At first, for instance, they will find that throwing a ball is easier than catching, unless the ball is big; children tend first to catch with their whole arm and not their hands. It will soon become clear that some children have particular talents – for example, they may have an especially good sense of balance or skill with a football.

The over-5s will run, climb, dance and jump about. They may combine all of these into some hair-raising stunts. They can skip with their feet and can learn to skip with rope, although boys may be convinced that this is just for girls. Some 6- and 7-year-olds may be able to ride a two-wheeled bike but many children still need the stabiliser wheels. Not all children learn to ride a bike: some never manage the necessary balance.

By 7 and 8 years old children have developed more confident balance. Given the opportunity to try out gymnastic equipment, they may be able to walk narrow planks. Their dancing has more rhythm and coordination. They may learn sequences of dance and movement to music and enjoy performing these.

With your encouragement and the chance to practise, a whole range of physical activities and games become a real possibility for the over-5s – trampolining, gymnastics, or swimming; even the beginnings of diving.

Fine coordination

The improvement in skills needing fine coordination is noticeable in children's ability to take care of themselves by this stage. Dressing and undressing, managing in the toilet and eating meals fairly neatly all require coordination of hand and eye. Children need to concentrate if they are to follow through a sequence of related movements.

Children of 6 and 7 draw and paint with plenty of detail as they depict people, buildings or transport. They will probably have some favourite subjects that they prefer to draw.

You can encourage all children in interests that may develop into hobbies. Some children will show a flair in particular activities: they may become especially expert and enthusiastic builders, or may relish model-making or needlecraft.

Children at this age are learning to write – a difficult skill that needs coordination of hand and eye. Children who can draw with pencils and crayons are learning to make the patterns that will form writing. They need to move from a whole-hand grasp to a finer fingers-and-thumb hold; some children find this harder than others. They also need to have developed a clear right- or left-hand preference. (Section 5.3 gives more detail on learning to write.)

Children with difficulties

Children do sometimes mock those who are clumsy or slower in physical games. You may need to be firm in stopping any teasing and to make sure that the choice of games does not favour only the speedy or best-coordinated of the children.

Just as with the younger age range, there may be particular limits for children with disabilities. You need to make sure that children are no more limited than is absolutely inevitable. Children with disabilities that affect their senses or their physical coordination will still want to explore and develop these skills with their friends.

ACTIVITY

1 If you watch, you will be able to see how 5- to 7-year-olds are more able to plan what they will do. By asking a few simple questions, you can encourage a child to think ahead before she starts. For example:

- 'What do you want to write about?'
- 'How will you stick the cardboard to the base?'

2 Children are also more able to consider the reasons that a project has not gone as well as they expected. In conversation, you can help children to think over, for example:

- 'Why did my model collapse?'
- 'How would I do it differently next time?'

Physical disabilities and development

One of the most common causes of physical disability is that the body's central nervous system has been damaged. There can be many different reasons for this damage: you cannot generalise about children with disabilities, even those who share a specific disability.

For example, children with cerebral palsy have difficulties with movement, balance and coordination. Perhaps they will have hearing or visual problems. They *may* have an intellectual impairment, but not necessarily.

Children with physical disabilities may benefit from physiotherapy. Some children will achieve mobility with the help of callipers, leg gaiters or a wheelchair. An occupational therapist can advise on these mobility aids, as well as how to make a nursery or playgroup more accessible.

For your information

You will need further advice if you are caring for children with physical disabilities. We have given suggestions for books and some useful addresses in sections 3.4 and 5.1; you could also use these:

★ Advisory Centre for Education 1992: *Special Education Handbook*, 5th edn.

★ Jeffree, Dorothy and Roy McConkey 1993: *Let Me Play*, revd edn. In the 'Human Horizons' series (Souvenir Press).

4.2 Enjoyable and safe activities for children

This section concentrates on the activities that will help children develop their physical skills. You will be free to enjoy the time with children if you are confident they are safe.

It will be helpful if you look at other sections of the workbook together with this section:

- Section 2.5, on organising children's environment;
- Section 2.6, which will remind you how children learn best;
- Section 3.3, which covers teaching children to take care of themselves – rules for safety and learning everyday tasks which are linked to the development of physical skills.

Children's environment needs an element of challenge otherwise they will not extend their physical skills. Children should be as safe as you can possibly manage; but you should recognise that some children unfortunately will still have accidents, even in an environment that has been planned for them.

The following activities will help you think about combining challenge with safety.

Crawling babies can move fast

ACTIVITY

Babies can develop new physical skills almost without warning. For example, a baby who has been lying quietly on her back while you change her will learn to turn from her back to her side. If you are not ready for this, she could tip herself off the changing mat. This could be dangerous if she is being changed on a table.

Look carefully at the arrangements you have for:

- changing babies;

- sitting babies up so they can see what is going on;
- putting them on a rug or blanket on the ground so that they can move in safety.

1 What arrangements might only be safe while a baby lies on his back?
2 Some active babies bounce a lot. Can they make the baby seat move?
3 How fast can a baby move by rolling?

TO THINK ABOUT

You will sometimes take a group of children out of your centre or school. New ground rules are usually needed.

Imagine that:

- you are in charge of three children aged between 5 and 7 years and you are all in a park;
- there are trees, an unfenced pond and an enclosed play area;
- the park is large enough that you cannot see the boundaries from where you are.

1 What rules would you establish with the children?
2 How far away could you let any one child wander?
3 What play equipment might you take with you?
4 How might you use the play experience for chatting later?

Playing games

Children need space to move around freely. However, they also enjoy quiet corners for looking at books or imaginative play. They like to get into safe small spaces like a home corner or cardboard boxes and home-made tents.

Children need clean and warm floors as they often play sitting on the ground. Any floors, including any rugs, must be non-slip; children can skid easily. Crawling babies need a comfortable floor surface. You will appreciate this as well when you play with them.

She climbed up – but can she get back down?

Games with equipment

Look upon yourself as an extremely valuable piece of equipment. Children want a lively adult who is ready to join in with dancing sessions, organised games, running around and climbing.

Babies and toddlers will be delighted if you are willing to crawl around and be crawled over, jumped on and wrestled with. Wear comfortable clothes and if possible get some large foam mats for the floor.

By your involvement, you and your fellow workers may be able to counter stereotypes. For example, children may believe that girls and women don't play football or that boys and men don't skip.

You need to think about children's play clothes. For example, children with carefully plaited hair may need a head covering when they play with sand. Not all families may be happy for their children to strip down to underwear for lively games or dance. Some Muslim families, for instance, will require that their daughters keep their arms and legs covered, and probably their hair as well. Talk with parents to find a compromise of modest dress in which the girls can still enjoy the games.

As well as you and your energy and ideas, children also need a selection from the following:

- *Safe climbing equipment* – available where you work or through trips to good-quality play parks or adventure playgrounds.
- *Games equipment* – try to have a range, including different sizes of bats and balls, skipping ropes and hoops.
- *Smaller-scale games* – marbles, jacks and the like are fun for the over-5s.
- *Equipment to ride* – examples are bikes and pull-along trolleys.

Playing games

Even quite young children can organise themselves in games involving running, chasing and hiding. You can help them extend their games by laying out simple obstacle courses for crawling or bike-riding. You may be able to chalk out temporary markings for toy-car roadways or hopscotch for the older children.

They will appreciate your organisational and umpiring skills for other games. Children like games of throwing or rolling balls to each other and simple tennis or cricket with a soft ball. They need your arms for games with long skipping ropes in which the ends are held by turners.

Children can enjoy an organised physical game as much as playing with their friends without an adult. The over-3s will cope with being organised so long as the rules of the game are not too difficult. Few under-8s will put up with waiting around too long for a turn at a game. Before you start, you need to be clear about the rules: think about how you will explain them simply to children. Can you sort out a simpler set of rules so that younger children can enjoy rounders or football?

Some games have winners and losers and you will have to deal with this issue even if you organise mainly co-operative games. You can try to organise any teams so that one group of children is not regularly losing. Winners deserve to be congratulated for their efforts but you need to prevent lengthy crowing.

There are many possible games to play with children. You will remember some from your own childhood, and some party games are suitable. Keep an open list of good ideas.

Here are a few to start your list. You can change the wording in games as long as this does not confuse the instructions.

Simon says

Choose a leader. He gives instructions such as 'Jump up and down' but the group must only obey if the leader says 'Simon says . . .' first. If a child obeys *without* this phrase then he is out of the game.

Grandmother's footsteps

Choose one person to be grandmother; she then turns her back. The rest of the group moves about 5–6 metres away. The children creep up on grandmother. But she turns round frequently and suddenly, and any child who is seen moving has to go back to the beginning. When a child reaches grandmother, she takes her place.

Busy bees

The children form pairs. You call out different instructions that the children have to follow together, like 'Hold hands' or 'Face each other'. Now and then you call out 'Busy bees' and the children have to buzz as they find a new partner. You also try to grab a partner, and if you are successful the odd child out becomes the new leader.

Dragon head and tails

This game originates in China where dragons have great spiritual significance.

The children line up, each holding the shoulders of the child in front. The front child is the dragon's head and the back is the tail. At first the children stand still: the dragon is asleep. Then you shout 'Chase' and the head whips round to chase the tail, which in turn tries to keep out of the way.

All the children must hang on. If the head touches the tail, then the child who is the tail comes to the front. If the dragon breaks, then the head goes down the tail and the second in line becomes the dragon's head.

For your information

★ There are many more games in Gyles Brandreth's *Children's Games* (Chancellor, 1992).

Music and dance

Music should be available for all children and not just those who finally learn an instrument. Younger children enjoy making music by singing and using simple instruments. It may be noisy but it's fun. Give children experience of the music of different cultures and help them to appreciate what may be very different patterns of sound and different instruments.

Even babies can enjoy music. They often love to hear songs from you and to be danced around in your arms. Some toddlers will bounce in time to music and by 3 or 4 some children are good dancers.

Children of 3 years and older can be introduced to music and movement. Many enjoy moving at different paces in time with a piece of music and pretending to be animals or trees. If you are patient, they may learn a sequence to a piece of music which they will then proudly perform.

Creative work

All children will find creative activities that they enjoy and some will discover a real talent. Encourage them to experiment and persevere through any frustrations.

- Explain to children what you have laid out on a table and what they can do.
- Be ready to show an individual child how to do something, and to explain again if he does not seem to have understood.
- Help older children plan what they want to do in a piece of needlework or a model.
- Keep children company while they are working. You can be making something yourself, but don't do something so impressive that the children are daunted.
- Chat with children about their drawing or their construction when they have finished. Sometimes you will ask 'What have you made?' or 'What's in your painting?' Younger children may not have been painting a particular subject, so don't press them. You can chat about how well the colours or texture work.
- You need to be careful not to set unrealistic standards for children's creative work. However, children do not really benefit if they are praised regardless of their effort and the end-product, for example if a child has dashed off a piece of work without any care.
- Display children's work if at all possible and let them take some home.

Drawing and painting

Children learn to use different equipment like pencils, crayons, chalks and paint brushes. You can show them a wide range of techniques. This could include any of the following:

- sketches and paintings of children's own choice;
- colouring shapes and patterns;
- butterfly paintings, made by painting on half of a sheet of paper which is then folded over;
- prints made by placing paper onto water on which oil and paints have been floated;
- creating textures with different thicknesses of paint, perhaps mixed with other substances like icing sugar.

Children like to see displays of their work

Printing and dyeing

Even little fingers can manage simple printing with a thick paint mix and everyday objects like chunks of fruit or cotton reels. Children can make their own choice of pattern by pressing the shape onto paper or fabric.

Children can produce impressive tie-dyeing by using string, clothes pegs, corks or elastic bands to tie up cloth or old tee-shirts. You will probably have to do the actual soaking in the dye. Take care that children don't get dye in their eyes or on other parts of the body.

Collage, sticking and paper work

Children can be very pleased with what they produce in this craft. Collage also works well in combination with drawing and painting. Children can use paper, silver sweet-wrappings or milk-bottle tops, cloth, pasta or polystyrene shapes. Anything safe can be used that children can cut and stick.

Cutting with scissors is quite a difficult physical skill. You will provide blunt-ended scissors and these do not always cut easily. Children may learn more quickly if you provide polystyrene trays, like the packaging from supermarket-bought vegetables or meat: with these they can learn the movements for cutting, and the polystyrene does not bend like paper.

The over-5s may manage, with help, to make tissue flowers and flap or pop-up cards. The Japanese craft of origami offers simple as well as complicated designs for paper sculpture.

Collections

Even young children are often interested in collecting around a theme, such as leaves or pressed flowers, labels of food tins, stamps or postcards. They enjoy the collecting and you can help them lay out and stick items into a scrapbook or make a wall display.

Needlework and other crafts

Young children can make a start on crafts that adults enjoy. You help them by offering a simple version.

Many 3- and 4-year-olds enjoy needlework and you can introduce this safely. Start children with large-hole tapestry, called binca, and a blunt tapestry needle. Help them understand the basics of going down one hole and up another. If young children find this too difficult, then they could try sewing cards or patterns on polystyrene trays. Later, 4- and 5-year-olds can progress to sewing material together to make simple bags or wall hangings.

Children who have learned to wield a needle and thread can make some impressive items by threading tubular pasta. They can also use shells or nuts, but you will have to make the holes for them.

Weaving can be made relatively easy. You need a small weaving loom. You could make one by scoring each end of a piece of thick card and threading string around. Show children the basic technique of weaving under and over.

Knitting involves a number of coordinated actions that have to work together. It may be too difficult even for 7-year-olds. Those children who want to have a go need a project in which the final size and shape is not crucial. Watch all the time to check that needles are being used safely.

Construction and modelling

Even toddlers enjoy making things with playdough. Older children make models, pots and pretend food. If they wish to keep what they have made, you can let it dry out naturally.

Children can make impressive figures, machines or buildings out of junk materials, all of which will be free. The models can then be painted or decorated using the other creative arts.

You have a very wide choice of constructional play material. If you are on a tight budget then first buy wooden or plastic bricks of different sizes and some that fix together, like Lego or Duplo. If you have sufficient funds then you can choose different constructional sets to suit children from toddlers to 7-year-olds and still offer interest and a challenge to them. Younger children build towers and bridges. The over-5s may plan and build complex machines and complete landscapes and towns.

Children enjoy woodwork. You need to supervise this closely even if young children are not allowed the potentially more dangerous tools.

Observing children's involvement

All children need the exercise and satisfaction of using their physical skills. They will have favourite activities and you should not push them into something which they really do not want to do. However, watch out for unhelpful limits to what children can try.

Building confidence

Do you notice a child who lacks confidence in his physical skills? Can you simplify the physical task to encourage him to try? If he manages, get him to do it again, so that he feels more sure of his ability.

Notice your assumptions

Be aware of your own assumptions. Are you not surprised if the girls seem less adventurous? Are you letting some boys spend most of their time in vigorous activity, assuming that they will not manage a quieter or sit-down game?

Involving everyone

Watch out in mixed age groups that no age group is effectively being left out. For example, if you work in a club that has over-8s, you need to make sure that the 5–8s have activities that are at the right level. Watch out that these younger children have a part to play any group activity and are not pushed out by older children.

Similarly, in a nursery or playgroup, 3-year-olds can become frustrated if activities are more appropriate to the skills of 4- and 5-year-olds. Of course, the reverse can happen as well.

Abilities and disabilities

Take a careful look at the abilities of a child who has some disabilities. Is he being unintentionally excluded because he cannot hear instructions called out in a noisy room? Does she feel daunted because she fails to grab materials in an energetic free-for-all?

For your information: resources

You will find more ideas in many general craft books. The following publications are written with small fingers in mind.

★ Longman publish a crafts series with books on printing and junk modelling amongst others.

★ Usborne has the 'You and Your Child' series which has good ideas for playdough.

★ Michael Grater has compiled books on modelling, *Fun Models*, *Fun Figures* and *Fun Faces*, published by MacDonald.

★ For older children, the 'Fresh Start' series published by Franklin Watts has books on collage, puppets and the use of crayons.

For your information: playdough

Playdough is a versatile material for modelling. This is *our* favourite recipe, courtesy of Childsplay in South London.

★ Mix together in a large saucepan:

- 2 cups of plain flour;
- 2 cups of water;
- 1 cup of salt;
- 2 tablespoons of cooking oil;
- 2 teaspoons of cream of tartar;
- food colouring or powder paint for chosen colour.

Cook over a low heat, stirring continuously until the mixture is well blended and has thickened. Allow to cool before use.

★ The oil makes the mixture very pliable; the salty taste, as well as preserving the mixture, discourages children from eating the dough. The dough will keep for at least a couple of weeks in a plastic bag in a fridge.

5 The development of communication

5.1 Learning to communicate

What is communication?

Young children learn to speak one or more languages. They learn the accent and form of the language of those whom they hear. They also learn how they are expected to talk to other children and to adults. They may learn to have conversations; however, the experience of some children teaches them that it is not worth the effort to try to talk with adults.

Children can learn to listen carefully, but won't do so if the adults whom they copy do not listen to them. Children also learn about interrupting – whether this is allowed, whether it is worth waiting, and whether adults have different rules for children than for themselves.

Children watch your face as well as listening to your words

The unspoken messages

However, communication is more than learning to speak and to listen to actual words: babies and children are also very alert to body language. They are aware of *how* something is said as well as *what* is said. They watch the faces of others for their expression and they are alert to gestures that help them understand what has been said. Babies and toddlers depend on body language for a lot of the meaning of communication.

You may underestimate how much children notice the messages that are sent by your facial expression and your gestures. Many adults assume that, if nothing is said, children will be unaware of adults' feelings or worries. In reality, children who know you well will realise how you're feeling from your body language and general changes in your behaviour. Younger children may not be able to explain what they feel from you but they will still have noticed.

Body language and culture

Children learn the rules of body language for their own culture. You need to be aware that there are many cultural differences in body language; this could be important in your relations with children and their parents. A few examples follow.

Gestures do not send the same message around the world

For instance, in America you might beckon someone to you by extending your hand and curling your index finger back and forth. In England you would probably use this gesture only to a child. In Indonesia you would use the same gesture only to an animal – it would be considered rude to gesture like this to a person.

There are cultural differences in how close you stand to another adult

Americans typically stand about one arm's length apart. Japanese tend to prefer a greater distance. People from the Middle East and some South American countries prefer to stand much closer, perhaps even touching. You will notice individual differences within cultures on this comfortable distance.

Eye contact

English and American children are usually taught to look directly at an adult; this is reinforced with words such as 'Look at me when I'm talking to you.' If a child will not do this, adults tend to assume either that he is not concentrating or that he is guilty about something. However, children in many countries of the Far East, Africa and the Caribbean are taught *not* to look directly at adults: to do so would be judged disrespectful and impolite.

The development of communication 0–7

Babies – the first year of life

Babies' need for communication

You make contact with very young babies by soft words, looking and by touch. You need to hold babies close since they respond to a familiar smell and affectionate holding.

Babies are often soothed by your gentle conversation – probably as you deal with all their physical needs. It doesn't matter what you say: they will like the sound of your voice and look for your smile.

Babies who can't talk will still tell you how they feel

ACTIVITY

Suggestions for brief observations:

1 Spend some uninterrupted time watching a baby no older than 6 months of age. What feelings does she *seem* to be expressing through her face and how she moves her body? You are guessing, of course, but what does it look like?

2 Try to find a quiet corner and time of the day. Make a short tape-recording of you and a baby chatting together.

Play the tape later and listen for the different kinds of sounds that he is making. Is he joining sounds together? Does he seem to be copying any of the sounds you make?

Through caring for them, you get to know individual babies. You become more able to guess what they are feeling by the pattern of their cries and chuckles, and also through their body posture and facial expression.

Babies' own communication
Newborn babies have to communicate through crying. However, even their cries can vary from a quiet whimper to a piercing wail. Within a few months, babies become able to express their feelings and wants through different cries and other sounds, and by smiles.

As well as the sounds they make themselves, babies become aware, from the early months, of familiar voices around them. They come to recognise patterns of sounds associated with their daily routine. They are curious about unfamiliar sounds and may be startled by sudden, loud noises.

By 6 months of age, babies are producing a whole range of sounds. Their ability to communicate is part of their play. They will enjoy copying any sounds you make; they experiment with sound combinations and trills of sounds in a tuneful way. Babies will enjoy sound games with you, but sometimes you will hear them happily babbling by themselves as they lie in their cot.

From 6 to 12 months, babies deliberately experiment with both sound and body movements to support the simple messages they want to get across. They can call for your attention by shouts as well as crying. They will express their disapproval of food, or of part of their routine they don't like.

By the time they are a year old, babies show that they understand simple messages that you communicate by words and gestures. They will enjoy playing 'Say bye bye' or 'Clap hands'. They may hand over something when you request them to 'Give it to me'.

Babies will look up to the sound of a familiar name. Even if they cannot say the name themselves, they look for the person. They will recognise a few everyday names of objects in context. They may look in the right direction for 'Where's your cup?' or 'Where are your shoes?' Babies will understand a firm 'No!', although they may not be pleased about it.

From 1 to 2 years

What they can say
Toddlers of 12–18 months use expressive sounds and firm gestures to communicate with you. You will hear and understand a growing number of real words in their speech. They will get some of these words more or less correct first time; many others, though, will be in their own versions.

If you spend time with children of this age you become tuned in to what they are saying and how they say it. You use their gestures and facial expression as extra clues – just as *they* still do in order to follow what *you* are saying.

Toddlers often enjoy simple and repetitive rhymes or songs. These are even better if there are gestures that go with the words. They will listen, and may start to join in. You don't have to have an impressive singing voice – toddlers are just happy to hear you sing.

It is realistic for you to expect words and short phrases from toddlers by their second birthday. Children vary in this development and some are close to 2 years before they say much at all in real words.

Understanding what others say

Toddlers use the clues from knowing their usual routine and from the knowledge they have gained of what you usually want.

For example, suppose that an 18-month-old hears the word 'shoes' and sees you looking around. He will probably guess that your message is 'Where are your shoes? Will you help me find them?' On the other hand, suppose that he hears the word 'dinner' and you are in front of him with a spoonful of food and a firm expression on your face. He will probably conclude that your meaning is 'Stop messing about and eat your dinner now.'

From 1 to 2 years, toddlers are learning to follow simple instructions communicated by word and gesture. They often enjoy games of bringing you or pointing at familiar objects or toys, finding games such as 'Where's your teddy?' or 'Where's your nose?'

Toddlers are fairly willing to repeat their message if you don't understand. You can help them by being ready to repeat yourself in a slightly different way. Use helpful gestures and be prepared to show them what you want.

Young children make contact with each other

From 2 to 4 years old

Children's speech

Between 2 and 3 years, children usually learn more and more words. You will notice variation between children. Many 3-year-olds may have a working vocabulary of two hundred or more words; some will use even more. Children combine their words in phrases and short sentences. They often chat to themselves in play or talk out loud if they are struggling with an activity.

You will notice that young children are learning to use their speech for a range of purposes. They can call for your attention. They tell you what they want and what they don't want. They like to tell you and show you things of interest. They will start to ask questions. At first these will be 'What?' questions, but they will grow to include 'Where?', 'When?' and 'Why?'

Children will make mistakes in their pronunciation of words and in how they put sentences together. You can repeat a word or phrase back to children so that they can hear the correct version. If children are having particular trouble with a word, be ready to help them practise if they want. Offer this help with affection and without negative criticism.

Some children in your care may speak differently to you because of how their families speak. Some children will not have the same accent as you, or will order their words differently. You should not correct children to your way of speaking when they are talking in the same way as their families. They may, of course, be speaking a language which you cannot speak; we return to bilingualism in section 5.2.

Children copy adults as well as other children in using speech. They can learn a habit of shouting or of speaking more quietly. They copy an accent, word order and, of course, body language.

Body language

Children of 2–4 years will still use gestures to help carry their message. You can encourage them to repeat a message that you cannot understand or to tell you again in a different way. Sometimes you have to say 'Can you show me what you mean?'

Children still use your body language to make sense of your whole communication. They are learning a lot more about what adults in general, and you in particular, are likely to be asking – for example, you would want a used tissue put in the bin and not shoved in with the books. A familiar routine can help them.

Different sources of communication

Children of 2–4 years like to talk with an adult who will listen and show an interest. They become more able to hold a conversation and to take turns in talking and listening.

Children usually enjoy hearing stories – another source of words, phrases and ideas for conversation. You may read from a book with plenty of illustrations. They also enjoy storytelling from an adult who recounts a tale with lots of expression and gestures.

Children will enjoy rhymes and songs. They will learn many of these by heart and may enjoy performing in front of a group.

ACTIVITY

Children of 3 and 4 years should have many words. They use their vocabulary to communicate different kinds of messages.

Try to note down how one or two 4-year-olds use their speech in everyday conversation. Don't make your observation schedule too complicated. You could look at how often they use words in these ways:

- to *request* you or another child to do something;
- to *ask questions* (what words do they use? – 'why?', 'when?', etc.);

- to *describe* what they have done or their interests;
- to *retell* stories or rhymes that they have learned;
- to *explain* simply how something works, or otherwise to answer a question;
- to *speculate* in words as they wonder what might happen next or guess why something may have happened;
- to *justify* what they have done – this may be in argument.

---

4 years old and older

Words and ideas

By 4 years old children are becoming able to use words without an immediate link to something tangible. For example, if you ask 3-year-olds 'What's a ball?', they will probably look about for a picture of a ball or show you a real ball; 4-year-olds are more likely to understand that you want an answer in words. They may tell you that a ball is for playing football or that it bounces, or they may describe to you their own ball.

Take a moment and realise that these 4-year-olds have learned to use words to stand alone. They no longer need to point to the familiar object in order to talk about it.

By this time children use words flexibly to support their play. Some can vary their voice and choice of words to play a part in imaginative games; some will be embarrassingly good mimics of how familiar adults talk.

Using words in conversation

Younger children can talk about what is happening now, but 4-year-olds will tell you about past and future events. Of course, their time perspective is different from yours: they will give a different meaning from your own to words like 'soon', 'yesterday' or 'long ago'.

Most 4-year-olds can hold a conversation with another child or adult with whom they feel comfortable. You need to show an interest, of course, in topics that interest the child.

In their imagination, children can be anyone they like

The over-5s

By the time children are 5 years old they have an impressive ability to communicate, compared with a baby or toddler. They still have a lot to learn and there will still be misunderstandings – but even adults misunderstand one another.

The over-5s should have a very large vocabulary: it would be a major project to try to list all the words they use and understand. They know enough to realise when words are new to them, and will ask you for the meaning.

Children's speech will be fluent and mainly correct according to the language they have heard spoken. Children will accurately produce the local accent or their family's accent, or move flexibly between the two. They are often interested in other languages if they have the opportunity to hear them. Some 5-year-olds are fluent in more than one language.

Children aged 5 and 6 will be able to pronounce the majority of the sounds of their language. A few problems with sounds are not unusual; in English, for example, the more difficult sounds tend to be the groups of 's', 'f' and 'th', and 'r', 'l', 'w' and 'y'.

ACTIVITY

1   Tape-record, or video if you can, some 5- to 7-year-olds as they tell you about a subject that interests them. Their topic could be a favourite book, for example, or 'The best trip ever'.

2   Enjoy the recording with them afterwards. It is important that the children have fun: make sure that they do not feel criticised in any way. To be fair you could get somebody to record *you*, so that the children can enjoy *your* 'ums' and 'ahs' as well.

Your aim is to learn more about how these 5- to 7-year-olds use their words to express opinions and ideas.

Please remember the proper use of recordings like these: don't let anyone else listen or watch later unless the children have given their permission. Erase any recordings unless you can keep proper control of their use.

Reading on . . .

You might enjoy looking at these:
★   Axtell, Roger 1991: *Gestures – the do's and taboos of body language around the world* (John Wiley).
★   Morris, Desmond 1977: *Manwatching* (Triad Panther).
★   Petrie, Pat 1989: *Communicating with Children and Adults* (Hodder & Stoughton).

5.2 How you can help

Always remember that your help is both in what *you* say (your talk) and your response to what *children* say (your listening and looking). Children, even very young ones, will lose interest if an adult expects them to be the ones to listen quietly for the majority of the time.

With babies and toddlers

Toddlers learn to talk because adults have talked with them, long before they were able to say any recognisable words. Whatever language a baby will eventually speak, the following ways of behaving by an adult will help the process.

Be close

Look at babies and listen to what they have to communicate long before these are real words. You have to be close to a baby or toddler so that they can see your face. They want to look at you and probably touch you as well.

Let your face be expressive

You need to show babies that you are *enjoying* their communication. Your face communicates with smiles and looks. Your facial expression will also tell babies that you are waiting for something from them: when you say something, wait for the baby to reply, looking all the time. They will be confused if you say something and then turn away.

Use variety in your voice

You can let your voice be expressive – it helps if it is a bit larger than life. Babies will enjoy it if you play around with different sounds. In your chatting with them vary your volume sometimes, from normal loudness to whispering. This game will catch their attention and probably amuse them.

Slow down a little

It makes sense to speak more simply and a little more slowly than you would to an adult or an older child.

Leave a clear pause at the end of each sentence. This gives a baby or toddler the opportunity to say something.

Keep your words simple and your sentences short. Emphasise your words with lots of expression. You might use children's own words for a person or object sometimes, but don't make this your whole way of talking.

Be ready to repeat

It helps if you repeat the same message in different ways. For example, 'Where's your shoe? Can you see your shoe? Yes, there it is. Your shoe's on your foot.' You also help toddlers by repeating and simply expanding what they have said. For instance, he says to you, 'Mama coat', and you reply, 'Yes, that's Mummy's coat.'

When children have learned to talk

Be close enough

You still need to be close in order to look at children in a friendly way. Don't insist that they look at you, but be as close as they wish. Remember the cultural differences described earlier in section 5.1.

Children are shorter than you. Sit with them or bend at the knees so that they can look directly at you and not upwards all the time.

In a group it is particularly important to be close to young children when you are speaking. In a busy room, they may not realise that you are talking to them. Use names or a gentle touch to get children's attention before you start to talk.

The effort to understand children

Listen carefully to what children have to say, and give them time to think and then to express their opinions and thoughts. You may notice that some adults have developed bad habits of speaking to children and then looking away when the child is speaking.

If you won't listen, children may go to extremes to get your attention

If you do not understand what a child is trying to say, then it can help if you tell them so directly. You may use other strategies such as saying 'Pardon' or asking children to repeat something, and some adults guess what a child means or start asking questions detective-fashion: it is much simpler and often more effective to say, 'Sorry – I don't understand.'

Be aware of how you talk with children

When you are talking about an activity, make clear the link between what you are saying and what young children are doing or can see at this moment. By 3 or 4, children are becoming more able to chat to you about events that are not actually going on in front of your eyes – for example, they may tell you about what they had for dinner last night. Even if you are talking with older children, be ready still to show as well as tell. You need never stop supporting by your gestures what you are saying in words.

With younger children you need to keep your sentences short and any instructions in a simple form. However, even over-5s can get confused if you give complicated instructions. It is a good habit to ask children to tell you in their own words what they think you want them to do: you will unravel a lot of confusions in this way. The repetition will also help them remember.

Alternative means of communication

If you are working with a group of staff, it is very useful if one person can communicate through sign language. Children with hearing loss may be learning to sign. Children with disabilities that affect language development sometimes learn signing together with spoken words. There is more about disabilities and language development later.

Learning two or more languages

Probably well over half of the world's population use at least two languages within everyday life. Many families resident in Britain speak another language in addition to English.

English as a language has developed over many centuries, enriched by the arrival of many different peoples. The wide range of sources for words is one reason for the difficulties in spelling. Separate languages like Welsh and Gaelic have continued to be spoken and written, despite some fierce attempts in the past to suppress them. (The Irish and Scottish languages are both called 'Gaelic', and the name is written that way. However, the latter is *pronounced* as if it were written as 'Gallic'.) Cornish did not survive as a spoken language and only exists now in the written form.

The twentieth century has seen the arrival of many other languages within the British Isles. Families have come to live in Britain from Asian, African, European and Far Eastern countries. Britain remains a multilingual nation but the different languages are unevenly distributed: in some parts of the country, English is the major or only language you will hear.

The British Isles are also a rich source of different versions of English. There are some wide variations in accent and pronunciation. There may also be dialects – different local words and sentence constructions. Combined, these can sometimes make communication difficult between people from different parts of the country. The arrival of families from the West Indies has added another version of English with its own history and traditions.

Helping bilingual children

The under-8s can and do become bilingual. They may be learning two languages simultaneously as they learn to speak; alternatively, they may learn one language within the family and then start to learn a second as they enter a new situation like nursery school.

You can help children by taking a positive approach to bilingualism, seeing it as an asset. However, you still need to recognise that learning any language is hard work for children. They aren't helped by the misplaced idea that they just 'pick up' a second language. Children need your help in the following ways.

All languages should be respected

Make sure that any language spoken by children in your care is respected.

For example, you may need to deal firmly with claims that Nazmin sounds funny when she speaks in Urdu, or that Susan is odd because she is more comfortable talking in English in a largely Welsh-speaking group.

It's easier to learn in your mother tongue

Children may be best helped by joining a group in which their first language is spoken fluently. If this is possible, they can learn their second language as part of the group experience. This approach, sometimes called 'mother-tongue teaching', may not be available, however. If it isn't, they may have to try to grasp complicated ideas (for example, see Chapter 6) through a language in which they are not yet confident.

Fluency depends on practice

Children need plenty of practice in a language before they become fluent. Encourage them to speak and build up their confidence.

Try to learn something of their languages

If you don't speak a child's most fluent language, show the effort in return of trying to learn some words and phrases from her.

Make allowances for their difficulties

Children may be able to handle a wide range of ideas in their first language, but not yet be at that stage in their second. Whilst they are learning, be ready to simplify your language and be willing to repeat yourself. Make sure that what you are saying is directly relevant to the situation in front of children. This will make life easier for them as they are learning.

Avoid confusion

Unless young children are equally confident in two languages, they can be confused if there is not a predictable pattern of who speaks which language and where. Older children have a greater understanding of the world and may themselves switch with ease between languages, even in mid-sentence.

Language in play

Children need the opportunity to talk and play with fluent child speakers as well as adults. Adults and children use any language in different ways.

Reading on . . .

You will find it useful to look at the following publications:

★   Arnberg, Lenore 1987: *Raising Children Bilingually – the pre-school child* (Multilingual Matters).

★   Saunders, George 1988: *Bilingual from Birth to Teens* (Multilingual Matters).

★   Blenkin, G. and A. Kelly 1992: *Assessment in Early Childhood Education* – the chapter on bilingualism and assessment (Paul Chapman).

Books for children in different languages

Two kinds of books are available:

• *Children's books written in languages other than English*   These can be stories from other countries or may be favourites, like the Spot books, translated into different languages. You may need to track these down.

- *Dual-language books*   In these, the same story is told in two languages; the writing runs in parallel.

It is worth borrowing or buying a small selection, even if your group speaks only one language. The over-5s will be interested in other languages and scripts, and these open up their horizons on the world.

For your information

★   Some of Peter Heaslip's 'Terraced House' series (Methuen) are dual-language. The 'All About Me' series (Blackie) has dual-language versions.

★   Magi Publications offer a range of stories, picture books and picture dictionaries. You can find out more by writing to them at 55 Crowland Avenue, Hayes, Middlesex UB3 4JP.

★   A useful address for you will be Multilingual Matters, Bank House, 8a Hill Road, Clevedon, Avon BS21 7HH (*tel*: 0275 876519). This company publishes a long list of books and journals about bilingualism; some of the titles are written for early-years workers and for parents.

Books and stories

Stories and pictures can be a great stimulus to language, both before and after children have learned to read.

Choosing books

There is a tremendous array of books for the 0–8s and children need access to a selection. How many you buy will depend on your budget. However, borrowing from a library will not only extend the choices but encourage children in the habit of using this facility.

You need these kinds of books:

- *Hard cardboard or material books*   You need books that will survive tough use by babies and toddlers. Less robust books can be kept on an upper shelf or special cupboard and brought out for supervised looking. Pop-up or flap books – for example, Janet and Allan Ahlberg's *Jolly Postman* (Heinemann) or Jan Pienkowski's books, such as *The Haunted House* (Heinemann) – will not survive vigorous handling.
- *Books for looking at and talking about*   Some books may have no words at all, for example Jan Ormerod's *Sunshine* and *Moonlight* (Picture Puffins).
- *Fiction – simple and more complicated stories*   Younger listeners like a straightforward tale with plenty of good pictures. They often enjoy a story line with a repeated phrase, for example Jill Murphy's *Peace At Last* (Picturemacs) or David McKee's *Not Now, Bernard* (Sparrow).
- *Non-fiction*   Children need access to some well-illustrated books about people, the world and how it works. There are suggestions in Chapter 6.
- *Poetry and stories with a poetic rhythm*   These can work very well if you deliver them with feeling. Examples are Michael Rosen and Quentin Blake's *Quick, Let's Get Out of Here* (André Deutsch) and the *Puffin Portable Poets*, a pocket-sized set of three books.

Conveying appropriate messages

Choose fiction that conveys the messages that you want communicated to the children. Remember, though, that children will not persist with books in which the message, however worthwhile, overwhelms the storyline. Always check for the quality of the tale, as well as making sure your whole selection of books or posters shows a world in which all kinds of people have a place.

Heroes can be boys and men but should equally often be girls and women. Take a careful look at what the male and female characters tend to do. Men should sometimes make the sandwiches or look after babies. Girls should sometimes be the leaders.

Some books set out deliberately to turn around stereotypes. Examples are Martin Waddell and Patrick Benson's *The Tough Princess* (Walker Books) and Tomie de Paola's *Oliver Button is a Sissy* (Magnet).

Some books work to engage children's interest in what they might view as boring adult stuff. For example, James Mayhew's *Katie's Picture Show* (Orchard Books) introduces children to paintings in an art gallery.

Depicting a racial mix

All children need books with characters who are of different races. Some of these stories may be set in countries other than Britain, but some should show the racially mixed communities that are part of Britain. Examples here are the 'Strands' series published by A & C Black; and the stories of individual children published by Hamish Hamilton, including *A Day with Ling* by Ming Tsou, and Joan Solomon's *Shabnam's Day Out*. Or try Iolette Thomas' stories about Janine (André Deutsch).

Making fun of people

Think very carefully before you use a book in which the physical appearance of a character is a source of comedy or pity.

Disabilities

Section 3.4 has suggestions for books with characters who have disabilities, and books which are informative about this topic.

Reading books to children

Before you read a book to a group of young children, you should know it well. You will not hold their attention well if you have to keep your nose in the book. Ideally, you want to be able to turn the book to the group so they can see the pictures with ease.

The over-5s may enjoy a longer book read day by day in episodes. You can then turn the book to them if there is an illustration. You should still have read the book to yourself before you read it to them: if you know what is coming, you are ready to discuss it with the children. Each day you can ask the children to say at what point you left the story and help them to remember. Stories by Roald Dahl or Graham Oakley's 'Church Cat' books, for example, can be enjoyed by children long before they could read the books themselves.

Children like traditional folk tales and religious stories as well as more modern fiction. For example, Anthony Horowitz's *Myths and Legends* (Kingfisher) gives a worldwide selection of stories. Always read folk tales to yourself before reading them out loud to the children: some are more racy or bloodthirsty than others.

The art of storytelling

Stories should not come only from books. Storytelling by word of mouth has a long tradition in many of the world's cultures; it can be most enjoyable for you and for children. You may have access to a good local storyteller, but don't see storytelling as a specialist skill.

The advantages of telling stories are that this is more immediate and personal for the children, and that it makes a change from reading. You can be flexible in the direction that the story takes. You can also use your storytelling skills when it might be difficult to read a book, for example when you are on a journey with children or when you are stuck with an unexpected delay.

You can do any of the following.

- tell stories that you know by heart, which are in books in your collection;
- re-tell favourite tales or fairy stories with a personal twist or jokes for this group of children – for inspiration, look at some of Tony Ross's re-told fairy tales, such as *Goldilocks and the Three Bears* (Sparrow);
- once you gain confidence, you might make up your own stories;
- use plenty of gestures and exciting noises to involve the children. Use pauses and the questioning look, asking 'What do you think she should do?' or 'What will happen next?'

Reading on . . .

★   If you get the taste for storytelling, you will find some more ideas in Nancy Mellon's *Storytelling and the Art of the Imagination* (Element Books, 1992).

Communication in groups

The under-3s need personal attention if they are to learn to communicate. If you are caring for this age within a group, you need to be especially careful about how you behave and how you organise your day.

How noisy is your group?
Babies and toddlers will have a harder job learning to talk if individual voices do not emerge from a high overall noise level.

Do you get close to babies and toddlers?
They need you within grasping distance. You need to have babies and toddlers on your lap or in your arms. Or else you need to be sitting together – perhaps on the floor.

How many adults does a baby see in one day?
Babies like company and they like a bit of change. However, babies may be confused by too many adults, especially if they appear without any predictable pattern. Babies may then be less able to get attached to familiar faces.

Children talking in groups

A day with children, even a few children, is punctuated by interruptions and

---

ACTIVITY

Over a period of about a week, you could make the following brief observations.

1   Did you manage to have a conversation, even a short one, with every child in your care?
2   Which children are likely to approach you? Who tends to wait for your approach?
3   Did you get an idea of what tends to stop a conversation? Is it another child who want attention or an adult?
4   What subjects do children enjoy talking about?

changes in direction. This is normal, yet you do not want interruptions to get out of hand.

You need to teach young children to wait a moment if you are talking with another child. If you really have to interrupt what a child is saying, then you should apologise if that is what you would expect of her in similar circumstances. Then you can encourage her to carry on by reminding her of what she was saying.

You can ask children questions about what they did at the weekend, and so on, but recognise that they will almost certainly be interested in what *you* did as well. You can share events of interest without revealing your personal life inappropriately.

The over-5s sometimes enjoy a 'Show and tell' time of the day. Over a week everyone has a chance to tell the group something of interest.

You will encourage children by asking them for their opinions, for example about a trip, a book or a television programme. Again, children enjoy an exchange of opinions – what do you think of a new film or programme? You can give them the experience of disagreeing with another's opinion without this turning into a fierce argument.

When to worry

Children vary in when they say their first words or combine words in short phrases: you cannot put an exact age in months on such developments. However, you need to be aware of warning signs that suggest that children's development is not progressing well, even allowing for variations between children.

Very quiet babies or toddlers

Some babies are more peaceful than others but they should all be making some sounds. Babies use sight as well as hearing in communicating with you. You won't necessarily realise that a young baby has partial or even total hearing loss.

Babies with hearing loss still make sounds. However, they tend not to change to the more tuneful babbling that is usual by 8 or 9 months. You should be concerned if a baby is making only a few sounds after 8–9 months or if the sounds are not getting more varied. Talk with her parents and suggest a check at the clinic, where staff will attempt to test her hearing separately from her sight.

2-year-olds who do not talk

If you work with a group of children in which many have a delay in their language, you can come to believe that most 2-year-olds do not talk. This is not the case: most do. You should be worried if a child is over 2 years and the months are passing with no sign that he can talk. There could be a number of reasons and you need to discuss the matter with his parents.

2- and 3-year-olds who say little

Sometimes young children do not say much but adults do not worry. They claim that the child understands practically everything that is said to her.

Perhaps a 2- or 3-year-old child seems to understand mainly your gestures rather than your words. Then you should discuss with her parents what may be the reason. Perhaps you don't realise that she speaks another language at home in which she is at ease. If she has only the one language, then she may be at a stage of development more usual for a younger child.

You should make some careful observations of a child who says little of her own accord. You can explore how much she understands of spoken language by seeing if she can follow simple requests when you make no gestures to help her. (You may find this difficult since gestures are part of whole communication for everyone.)

ACTIVITY

You could collect four or five familiar toys and place them in front of a 3-year-old who seems to be relying on gestures a great deal.

Ask her 'Where's the doll?' and similar requests. Make sure that you look at her and not at the toys. See whether she can hand you familiar toys or objects if you ask her in this way.

Watch her and see whether she looks to other children in a group when you say something. Does she then copy what they do?

3- and 4-year-olds whom only familiar adults can understand

An adult who is at ease with children should be able to understand most of the speech of a 3- or 4-year-old whom he does not know. You need a short time to get used to how any child talks and you probably need to share a similar accent.

Some 3- and 4-year-olds, however, can be understood only by adults and children who know them very well. These familiar people tend to translate what the child expresses. You should not ignore this. Discuss your observations with the child's parents: their child may need some specialist help from a speech therapist.

Stuttering

It is uncertain why children stutter (or stammer – the words tend to be used interchangeably). Possibly about 5 per cent of children have a noticeable stutter, but the majority emerge from it and do not have a lifelong problem.

It is not unusual for 3- and 4-year-olds to go through a phase of stuttering. One reason may be that children of that age have a lot more to say than they can easily express. In a busy group they may feel even more under pressure: they may believe, probably with good reason, that they have only a little time before another child will interrupt.

You can help by the following actions.

- Be patient, listen to children and wait for them to say what they want. Stuttering can be made into a problem by adults who are impatient or who allow a child to be mocked.
- Speak more slowly and only ask one question at a time. You can thereby create a relaxed atmosphere for chatting.
- Encourage older children to think about what they want to say before they start to speak. Wait whilst they do their thinking.

Be ready to chat with his parents about a child's difficulties in fluent speech. Make time for this conversation especially if any of the following is the case, since the child probably needs to see a speech therapist:

- if the child stutters a great deal, the months are passing and she is not improving;
- if she is really distressed by her stuttering and seems very lacking in confidence;
- if other members of her family have had problems with stuttering;
- if she is developing physical habits that accompany the stuttering, such as twitches or eye-blinks as well.

For your information

★ Your local speech therapy department may be able to help you. Otherwise, try the Stammering Centre, Finsbury Health Centre, London EC1R 0JJ (*tel.* 071–837 0031).

Language development and disabilities

Children vary considerably in how early they learn to talk and in how they use their language skills once these are established. A lot depends on the experiences that children have. However, some children have a disability that restricts their ability to learn language and perhaps other skills as well.

Learning difficulties

It is not possible to generalise about disabilities, even if children have been diagnosed as sharing the same condition. For example, children with Down's syndrome will have learning difficulties but the pattern is very varied. Children with cerebral palsy or spina bifida may have associated disabilities, for example with vision, but not necessarily.

Different methods of helping the children will be essential. In general, the children will benefit from patient help at a slower pace.

- *Make careful observations* Talk with parents and use your skills of observation to build an accurate picture of the child's current abilities.
- *Offer suitable activities* Adjust play activities to the child's level of development rather than his age in years and months. Be ready to make an everyday task or an activity more simple. Break a sequence, like making a jigsaw or eating a meal, into smaller steps, and help the child learn each step.
- *Offer routine* Children with learning difficulties may need a predictable routine even more than the other children. They may be more easily upset if what they expect is changed without warning.
- *Be realistic but positive* Keep realistically positive about children's development. A generation ago few people would have believed that any child with Down's could learn to read. Some children, with very patient help from their parents and workers, have proved this expectation wrong.

For your information

Useful addresses:
★ Association for Spina Bifida and Hydrocephalus, 42 Park Road, Peterborough PE1 2UQ (*tel.* 0733 555988).
★ Down's Syndrome Association, 155 Mitcham Road, London SW17 9PG (*tel.* 081–682 4001).
★ Spastics Society, 12 Park Crescent, London W1N 4EQ (*tel.* 071–636 5020).

Problems with hearing

Some children may have intermittent hearing loss. If children have a succession of heavy colds with ear infections, they may develop a condition known as glue ear. This can reduce hearing ability. Children may not tell you that they are in difficulties because they do not know – life to them is sometimes fuzzy and adults tell them off for not doing what they are supposed to do.

Children can be fitted with a hearing aid. However, aids tend to amplify all sounds and children may have particular difficulties in a noisy group. Children may find the aid physically uncomfortable in the ear. Watch out also for any teasing by other children. Children suffering the effects of glue ear may get some relief if grommets are inserted.

A specialist teacher or speech therapist could help you learn a sign language, even if only a small range of signs.

Reading on . . .

★   The Pre-school Playgroups information sheet: *Helping the Hearing-Impaired Child*. This leaflet also has useful addresses.
★   Jeffree, Dorothy and Roy McConkey 1991: *Let Me Speak* (Souvenir Press).
★   To help children understand a silent world: Brearley, Sue 1989: *Talk To Me* (A & C Black). The author describes through pictures and simple text the different ways of communicating besides talking.

For your information

A useful source of more information is:
★   National Deaf Children's Society: 45 Hereford Road, London W2 5AH (*tel.* 071–229 9272).

5.3 Learning to read and write

Children enjoy books

Learning to read

By the age of 4, children may already be interested in the written word: they may want to write their name, for instance, and some under-5s recognise a few familiar words or the names of shops. Between their 5th and 11th birthdays, children should become fully competent in reading and writing.

Building up to reading

Reading is a complicated skill. Children need plenty of encouragement and they need to practise. They will be more likely to persevere if they have learned to enjoy books already.

Children often learn favourite stories by heart. Their first efforts in reading a book are often telling a story they know, rather than reading it word for word. There is nothing the matter with this: it gives children a lot of pleasure and storytelling is itself an enjoyable activity. However, make sure that 6- and 7-year-olds are steadily making the link between the written word and the spoken version. Encourage them to read out loud from a book that is less familiar.

Bear in mind that in any written language there are rules about the ordering of the blocks of words or characters. For example, do you read from left to right or vice versa? If children come from a bilingual family, the two languages may follow different sets of rules. Point this out to children if they do not realise quickly. (See section 5.2 for suggestions of books in different languages.)

ACTIVITY

There are practical steps you can take to ease children into the skill of reading. When you are working with them, try some of the following:

- In a small group of 4-year-olds and older, point sometimes with your finger to show the direction of the written material you are reading.
- Chat to children as you read and look at books. For example, 'Let's start at the beginning – here', 'Don't turn the page yet, I have one more sentence to read', 'There's your favourite picture, let's see what it says about it'.
- Show children that you, yourself, read and write. Make the effort to read a recipe out loud or to make a legible list or menu. Point out that writing is all around. It is not just in books and magazines. It is on packets of food and on shop fronts or road signs.

Methods of teaching children to read

You may not yourself be teaching children to read but you should know about the two main approaches of recent years. These are:

- the 'look and say' approach, also known as the 'whole word' approach;
- the 'phonics' or 'sound' approach.

Look and say

'Look and say' focuses on the visual side of reading. Children are encouraged to recognise whole words by sight. These are simple words initially, usually taken from children's everyday spoken vocabulary. The words are often put onto large cards. The method is sometimes linked with graded reading schemes which use those words that children have learned to recognise by using the cards. Children progress through more difficult levels in the books.

The advantages of 'look and say' are that children can build up a working knowledge of a range of words that they can then recognise in simple stories. Children feel encouraged because they have started to read. Because the words they practise recognising in written form are the words they use in speech, there is also a good chance that children can see a point to reading: it links in with spoken communication.

However, if this is the only method of teaching reading then children have to continue to learn whole words. As they become more able readers, children may have difficulty because they do not have a system for working out new and longer words.

Phonics

'Phonics' as a method focuses on the way that words are put together. It stresses the *hearing* side to the written language: children are taught how to 'sound out' words. This is not only sounding by letters of the alphabet – this would not help children since there are 26 letters in the English alphabet but 44 sounds that make up the words in the language. Some letters are sounded differently in different words, for example, the 'c' in 'cat' and the first 'c' in 'circle'. Also you can get the same sound in different ways, for example, 'fat' and 'phone'. Combinations of letters produce combination sounds, as with 'bl' and 'str', for instance.

The advantage of phonics is that you are showing children how sounds build into an entire word: they learn a system that helps them work out how to read new words. With practice children can apply this to new pieces of reading material.

There are disadvantages if you depend on phonics as the only method of teaching reading. It can be very heavy going to the struggling early reader. It can seem ages to children before they can read something smoothly.

Which method is better?

This is not an easy question to answer. When we were writing this workbook we consulted with teachers and educationalists: there is nothing like 100 per cent agreement. The most sensible approach seems to be that children need the potential advantages of each method.

When children are beginning to learn to read, the whole-word approach helps them to build up a working knowledge of a range of words. They can then recognise the words in simple stories, such as stories from reading schemes. If children have easy access to a choice of books, there is no reason for them to conclude that reading is only done from the scheme books.

As their reading skill grows, however, children need the approach of phonics to learn how sounds build up to form an entire word. They are then learning a system for deciphering new words as they meet them. This is important for children as they become more fluent readers, and choose their reading material from a wide range of fiction and non-fiction.

Children need confidence in sounding out words to themselves if they are to learn how to spell. They will have to manage this in order to compose their own work. A child cannot check the spelling of a word if she has no idea how it might be spelt.

Helping the reading child

If you are responsible for the over-5s, you may be working in co-operation with a teacher in schools, or you may be in an after-school club or holiday scheme, or you may be working in a residential home. Please adapt the suggestions that follow to your own work responsibilities.

Listen to children read

As well as reading to themselves children need to practise by reading to an interested adult. This is best done in daily sessions, perhaps lasting no more than five minutes. You can encourage and help them with words they can't read.

You can correct a child's mistakes, but make sure this does not get disheartening. Don't pick them up on everything – at least initially; but don't, of course, tell them a word was read correctly if it wasn't.

Let children point to words as they read them

Children at the early stage of reading can very easily lose their place on a page. As they get more confident, they can be gently discouraged from following every text with a finger.

Encourage expression

As their reading improves, 6- and 7-year-olds become able to put more expression into what they read. They learn to use commas and full stops as signals to pause.

Chat about the books

When children have read as much as they can, talk with them about the story. Get them to show you the pictures and ask what might happen next in the story.

Read to children

Keep on reading out loud to children even when they are able to read to themselves. The over-5s enjoy short stories and longer books read in episodes.

Learning to write

Getting ready

Before children can produce readable writing, they have to get the pencil to do what they want it to. They will learn and practise this skill by activities which are enjoyable for their own sake. For example:

- free-hand drawing and sketching with finer pencils or crayons;
- tracing;
- copying repeating patterns like 'V' shapes or waves;
- marking a route through a simple maze or road map;
- joining the dots in a picture outline;
- colouring in shapes or pictures;
- if under-5s want to write their name, make them a clear version that they can copy.

Writing takes great concentration

You should respect a child's right- or left-hand preference. In some skills, being able to use both hands is an advantage. In writing, however, a child does need to make a firm decision between hands.

Your writing

Any writing you do on displays or menus should be printed clearly. Use lower-case letters – 'a, b, c' rather than 'A, B, C' – except, of course, for the first letters of a name or at the beginning of a sentence.

If you know that spelling is not your strong point, then check words before you complete a display. Think positively – you can be showing children how to use a dictionary.

The over-5s may be interested in different scripts and alphabets. If some children come from bilingual families you may have more opportunity to organise displays in different languages.

A primary school made a 'welcome' poster from the languages spoken by staff, children and their parents

Children writing

Recognise that this is a hard skill to achieve. Most 5-year-olds have a large vocabulary for talking and understanding. Their frustration as they start writing is that they do not have a clue how to write all these words.

When children try to write, they have to *recall* how to write and spell a word: they have to dredge it up from memory. When they read, they have to *recognise* a word. Children often read words correctly that they are still spelling incorrectly in their own written work – they recognise the whole word when it is on the page in front of them, but they cannot recall it from scratch in order to write it out letter by letter.

In the early stages of learning to write children can get practice by copying short passages or poems. As they try to compose their own material, you will encourage them by letting children flow in their writing without making a big issue of correct spelling. As children become more confident in writing down their ideas, you should focus their attention on a few words at a time. You can encourage them to check whether a word looks right before telling them the correct spelling.

There are many ways to use writing and it will be helpful if children can join you in practical applications. You could involve them in any of the following. You don't have to wait until children are confident writers – let them have a go, with the spelling they can manage and with illustrations to supplement their message if they want:

- making shopping lists for trips;
- writing reminder notes for you or for the children themselves;
- writing plans for group activities;
- sending off for offers on packets, or material from children's television programmes;
- labelling posters and displays;
- preparing menus for the week.

Dyslexia

Some 7-year-olds and older have persistent difficulties in learning to read and write, although they have had plenty of time and encouragement from adults. Perhaps a child is still making a lot of mistakes; it looks as if he depends on illustrations to guess words. Even if he has in the end read words correctly, he is silent when you try to chat about the passage he has just read. It is possible that his learning problems are caused by dyslexia. (Although some girls are dyslexic, the majority of children with the condition are boys.)

Identifying dyslexia

As well as problems in learning to read, there is a pattern of difficulties that appear to be linked with dyslexia. Of course, none of these indicates dyslexia on its own. Watch out for:

- problems with the spoken language – children who are later in learning to talk and who have difficulty putting thoughts into words;
- some physical clumsiness in skills that need fine coordination;
- confusion over right- and left-handedness, at 5 or 6 years, when most children have established a clear preference;
- specific difficulties with the written word, writing letters backwards, and muddling similar-looking letters.

How to help

As with any other disability, the sooner dyslexia is identified, the sooner a child can be given special help. However, as a worker with the under-8s you may find that the specialist services in your area are resistant to making a diagnosis of dyslexia as yet.

You can best help by:

- sharing your observations with the child's parents, and finding out their views;
- making sure that your concerns are understood by workers who will continue to be responsible for this child;
- supporting a child who is having the kind of difficulties described earlier, and boosting his confidence in himself;
- encouraging an enjoyment of books through continuing to read aloud to a child who is not succeeding in learning to read to himself.

For your information

★   You can get advice and information from the British Dyslexia Association: 98 London Road, Reading RG1 5AU (*tel.* 0734 668271/2).

6 The development of thinking

6.1 Can you look through children's eyes?

Babies and children develop and change in the way that they make sense of the world around them. A 4-year-old will show you her ideas about the world through what she says and does. You will see that these are very different from those of 2-year-olds of your acquaintance; they are also noticeably different from those of 7-year-olds.

You will help children by watching them and listening carefully. Try to recapture, as far as possible, a view of the world through the eyes of a young child. Their mistakes will give you as much information about how much they understand as what they get right. You will probably find the process fascinating.

Babies and toddlers

Before young children can talk to you, you have to deduce what they understand of the world by observing what they do.

Watch babies within the early months and you will see them begin to discover the boundaries to their own bodies. Sometimes these discoveries are painful: a baby may chew on her own toe, for example, not realising that this is joined to her and that she will hurt herself.

By a few months of age, a baby will have discovered simple patterns of cause and effect. He may smile at a familiar face, for example, knowing that this often brings a smile in return. Nevertheless, he may unintentionally hit himself with a rattle, and his outraged expression and cries are very different from the emotions shown when he has done something deliberately.

By 6 months babies can tell familiar from unfamiliar faces and they recognise the sights and sounds of everyday routines. For example, if a baby enjoys bathtime then the sounds of a bath running will bring smiles and waving arms and legs. If she dislikes having her nappy changed, or just does not want to be confined at the moment, she will cry and struggle.

By 9 months old a baby will have learned that it is worthwhile searching for toys. Just because he can't see them, they haven't gone for good.

We have stressed in other parts of this workbook that toddlers are naturally very curious and can be extremely persistent in their explorations. Do remember that they have very limited understanding about the likely consequences of what they do. For example, an 18-month-old will not realise that objects flushed down the toilet cannot necessarily be retrieved.

Toddlers do not know enough to have a sense of danger. However careful you are, they will make some uncomfortable discoveries – hot things can hurt, pets sometimes scratch or bite.

Toddlers can remember people and places. They may recognise a route that they travel regularly on visits. They may get excited at the sight of the bakers, recalling that they often get a bun there. They remember the usual place that their toys are stored and where the biscuits or sweets are kept.

However, toddlers get excited and this can lead them to make exactly the same mistake that gave them the bruising yesterday. Even with 2- and 3-year-olds, a useful warning memory is often pushed out by curiosity.

SOME EXAMPLES

Reuben

14-month-old Reuben walks around his flat in the morning and points to the curtains which are not yet open. He waves at the closed curtains and makes firm noises until his mother or father opens them. In the winter evening, as it gets dark, he walks round, pointing imperiously at the ones which are not yet closed. He is content when the curtains are as they should be for the time of day.

Gemma

At 16 months old, Gemma has learned that some items belong to people. She picks up her father's slippers or his watch and clearly says 'Daddy'.

Zoe

Zoe, who is 18 months old, watches her brother who is crying. She does not say anything but she brings him his favourite toy monkey and his quilt. He is usually comforted by holding these objects. She does this on several occasions when nobody has asked her to do this.

Children of 2 and 3 years

Young children are learning the names of people and objects. At this age they are thinking in a concrete way; they link the meaning of words to a particular context. The word 'cup' is linked to a real cup, initially their own cup. The words 'Mummy' and 'Daddy' have been linked to real, unique people.

Some 3-year-olds are developing a grasp of ideas that can be expressed in words. The words for heat and cold are descriptions, for example; 'hot' does not exist as something you can hold up. Radiators are hot and dinner may be hot. People may feel hot – yet nobody can hold up a 'hot'. Colour words also are descriptions: you cannot have a 'blue' although you can have a pen that makes a blue colour; a child may have blue trousers or could collect a pile of blue bricks.

Already 2- and 3-year-olds have learned much about their own world. They may have learned to avoid some specific dangers about which you have warned them, but they do not have much idea of what else might be dangerous. Even regular warnings, for example about the danger of busy roads, may be completely forgotten if something or someone catches their attention. This is still true for older children.

Young children are very literal. You may warn a child not to run out in the road after his ball; he may conclude that it is safe to run out after something else.

Some concepts dear to the heart of adults are not immediately attractive to young children. For instance, a child may *remember* what you said yesterday about sharing toys, but she cannot see the point – especially as this one is her favourite.

Often 2- and 3-year-olds welcome some advance notice about what is going to happen and when within their day. Their understanding of time is basic, so they need this information in terms such as these: 'We will tidy up and then we will have a story. Then we will have some lunch.'

Remember that 2- and 3-year-olds have only a limited understanding beyond the present.

SOME EXAMPLES

Simon

Simon, who is 2 years old, has been enjoying a 'Thomas the Tank Engine' story in which one of the engines falls down a deep hole because he ignored a sign that said 'Danger – keep away'. Several days later Simon says to his mother, 'Scissors – you got them – it's danger – keep away me.'

Marie

Marie, 2 years old, makes jokes by saying something that she knows is wrong. She points to her grandmother and says, 'You baby Anna – no – just pretend'. One day she makes up the phrase 'hot sandwich' and laughs loudly.

Jerry

Jerry, 3 years old, is learning to put his feelings into words. His father has to go away for a week on a business trip. Jerry says on his return, 'We lost you Daddy and I cried.' His childminder gives away an old toy and Jerry says, 'I'm cross with you, 'cos that was mine.'

Anya

Anya, who is 3½, looks with concern on her face at a high tower block. She asks, 'Will that fall down?' Her father says, 'No, Anya. Why do you say that?' and Anya replies, 'My Lego towers fall down.'

Children of 4 years and older

Most 4- and 5-year-olds are grasping many different ideas, yet even when children are attending the same nursery or playgroup, they vary a great deal in what catches their interest. By the time they enter primary school, children will have the basis of many ideas.

Logical mistakes

> If you thought hard enough, he'd always considered, you could work out everything. The wind, for example. It had always puzzled him until the day he'd realized that it was caused by all the trees waving about.
>
> Masklin's thoughts in *Truckers*, p. 87 – the first of the 'Nome' trilogy, by Terry Pratchett (Corgi, 1989)

You will discover by talking with and listening to children that they still have a lot of confusion to unravel. However, they often think logically from what they know already. They make mistakes, but many of their mistakes are sensible deductions from their current state of knowledge.

You can learn a great deal by following the children's logic. You can then help them from the point they have reached.

Learning ideas

What follows is a brief checklist for you of the ideas that 5-year-olds are grasping. These are expanded, with suggestions for activities, in sections 6.2 and 6.3.

Colours

Children of 5 years should be able to recognise and name common colours.

Numbers

By 4 and 5 years of age children are learning the words for numbers. They have some grasp of the order of counting, '1, 2, 3, 4, 5 . . .', and can probably count up to 20 or 30. They can also count how many objects there are in a small group and they know that the counting stops when they have counted all the objects.

Time

By this stage children understand about different times of the day, for example lunchtime or going-home time from nursery or playgroup. They are very unlikely to be able to tell the time by a watch or clock. They have a general idea of past, present and future but their perspective on time is not an adult one.

The idea of measurement

Children of 4 and 5 years understand simple ways of comparing or measuring people and objects; they have ideas about overall size. They probably use descriptions like 'big', 'small', 'fat' or 'thin'.

They may have learned about different shapes. They may recognise and be able to name common shapes like square, circle, rectangle or triangle.

They will have ideas about height and weight although these may both be described by the word 'big'. They are gradually grasping the idea of relative height and weight.

The idea of opposites

Children at this age understand a number of ideas by extreme examples. For instance, they probably understand the idea of different temperatures by the opposites, hot and cold. Speed is a complicated idea for them to grasp, yet again they can probably understand the opposites, fast and slow.

The world around them

Even young children show an interest in the world about them. By 5 years of age children will have some ideas about events like the weather. They will be curious about plants and how they grow.

Understanding people and relationships

Children of 5 years will be aware of differences between people, such as different sexes or skin colours. They will have some understanding of families and family relationships, according to their own experience. They may be trying to grasp the meaning of jobs and work in adult life.

At this age also children have ideas about other people's feelings as well as their own. They may have some grasp of the meaning of birth – this is variable and some children are more interested than others. Depending on their experience, some children may have ideas about health and sickness or about disabilities. They may have a curiosity about growing up or growing old, or about death.

Imagining . . .

Reading on . . .

If you are interested to read more about how children learn to think, try:
★ Donaldson, Margaret 1978: *Children's Minds* (Fontana).
★ Grieve, Robert and Martin Hughes 1990: *Understanding Children* (Basil Blackwell).
★ Tizard, Barbara and Martin Hughes 1984: *Children Learning* (Fontana).

SOME EXAMPLES

Ramone

Ramone, who is 4, is telling his nursery worker that it is his birthday next week. She asks him how old he will be. Ramone says, 'Four. I'll be four.' He pauses and then says, 'Did you know? You have to be three and a half before you can be four?'

Matthew

Matthew, who is 4, has been watching a children's news programme on television. He asks, 'Why are the children hungry in Africa?' He waits for an answer.

Daniel

Daniel, who is 5, asks questions about Auntie Janet's very fat tummy. His mother explains that it is a baby growing inside her. Daniel wants to know how the baby can get food. A couple of weeks later he asks how the baby will get out of Auntie Janet. It is not until six months later that he asks a general question about how babies get into women's tummies.

Laura

Laura, who is 5, has been with her father to pay the newspaper bill. When they emerge from the shop she asks him, 'Why did the man give you money? You said we were going to pay him.' Laura has not understood the process of paying more money than is needed and getting change in return.

Making sense of the world

From Jennie Laishley's *Working with Young Children*, p. 101 (Hodder & Stoughton, 1987):

> When my son was four years old, he asked me . . . , 'Are my T-shirts getting smaller?' . . . I answered, 'No' . . . 'Well, am I getting bigger then? Because Zoe's got my red T-shirt now.' He was searching for an explanation of why his T-shirts now fitted his younger sister but not him. A world in which clothes get smaller would explain this just as well as one in which children get larger.

6.2 How you can help – early maths and science

Your general approach

You will help children learn by all of the following.

Be patient with them

Children are learning some complicated ideas: they will get confused sometimes. You can help by being ready to give your time and effort to work out what a child does not understand.

Repeat yourself

Be willing to go over the basics of an idea more than once. You will help children by offering a choice of activities that illustrate the same idea in different ways. Children's understanding will build up over time; don't expect them to grasp a complicated idea in one sitting. They need repetition and practice.

Look through the child's eyes

Many ideas and ways of describing the world are not obvious. They only seem obvious to you because of the many years that you have lived with these ideas.

Be ready to help if children get stuck

Get involved

Children warm to adults who get excited with them about new discoveries. You will find that children show you new insights – they come fresh to old ideas.

Sometimes they will be grasping an idea that is perfectly clear to you. Don't pretend that you were ignorant when you weren't, but do enjoy the delight of discovery with children. You can do this by asking them to share with you: 'What have you found out?' or 'What have you learned from this?' Compliment them for what they have discovered. Be generous with comments like, 'That's a new way of looking at that' or 'I wouldn't have thought of doing it that way, what a good idea.' Avoid asking children only questions to which you already have the answer. Make some genuine experiments: 'I wonder what will happen if we . . . ?'

Show as well as tell

Don't depend entirely on words to carry some complicated ideas. Help children by your choice of activities to illustrate ideas.

Helping with colours

Children are learning colour words as descriptions. The story of *Mr Rabbit and the Lovely Present*, by Charlotte Zolotow (Puffin Books, 1971), is built around this idea. The little girl wonders what to give her mother:

'Something that she likes is a good present,' said Mr Rabbit.
'But what?' said the little girl.
'Yes, what?' asked Mr Rabbit.
'She likes red,' said the little girl.
'Red,' said Mr Rabbit. 'You can't give her red.'

'Something red, maybe,' said the little girl.
'Oh, something red,' said Mr Rabbit.
'What is red?' said the little girl.
'Well,' said Mr Rabbit, 'there's red underwear.'
'No,' said the little girl, 'I can't give her that.'

Children of 5 should be able to tell the difference between common colours such as blue, green, red, yellow, pink or orange. They should also be able to identify the colours by the correct colour name. You might disagree about subtle shades, but adults argue about these too – some blues are very close to green, for example.

Learning colours is a two-stage process. First a child has to notice those differences in the world that you would describe by colour words. He has to recognise, by sight, the difference between red and blue. You learned this so long ago that you have probably forgotten how hard it can be – children have to distinguish colours from all of the other ways that an object could be described, such as the texture or the person to whom an object belongs. Once a child can tell the difference between colours he is ready to put a label to a colour. He can then practise identifying examples of a colour in clothing or toys.

Helpful play activities for 3- and 4-year-olds include these:

* sorting out a collection of bricks by colour;
* helping to tidy up when some toys are organised by colour;
* making collections for a display on the theme of colour;
* playing games in which colours are compared to decide whether they are the same or different.

You can help by being aware of the kind of question that you are asking children. For example, if you say 'Find me something red' or 'What colour is this truck?', then you are assuming that the child can identify colours. A simpler task is to ask the child to find another example of the same colour. You do this by asking, 'This is a red car. Can you find me another red car?' The child then has something to match.

If 4- or 5-year-olds seem to be confused about colours, play some very simple sorting games with them. Check out carefully whether they can see the difference. Then build up through matching games until you try the activities that give children experience in identifying objects by colour.

You should be concerned if children are still confused after some special help from you. They may need to be checked for colour blindness. Talk this over with their parents. Colour blindness is more common among boys than girls. Children or adults who have some level of colour blindness do not necessarily live in a world that looks grey. Some have a difficulty only with certain parts of the colour spectrum.

Helping with numbers

Mathematical ideas are another way of describing the world. You can see them as a convenient shorthand that helps anybody describe more specifically ideas such as more or less and how many.

The under-5s

Children are learning to handle numbers before they enter primary school. You can use play activities to help young children learn the basic ideas that build into mathematics.

Children need practice in counting how many. This can be almost anything, for example:

- 'How many children are here today? So how many cups do we need?'
- 'How many cars are there in the box?'
- 'How many ducks are there on the lake?'
- 'How many dots are there in this pattern?'
- 'How many apples are there in the bowl?'

Listen to children counting, as high as they wish – there is nothing the matter with this; they are learning the order in which numbers come. Make sure that they also get practice counting a fixed number of things: you can ask children to fetch you 'two plates' or 'four more crayons'.

Counting up real objects moves naturally into counting how many there are once some have been added or taken away. Some songs and rhymes are good practice. Children can also play with toys where you add one or take one away and get them to count. Simple shopping games or actual trips to the shops help with practical uses of number skills.

Cooking and some craft activities provide enjoyable experience in simple measuring and in comparing lengths, sizes or weights. Meal-times and play in the sand give opportunities for learning simple fractions as a cake or a sand pie is divided up.

Games with cards and board games can be a practical help. Children get practice in counting their way around a board and in counting up the dots on large dice. Games like dominoes are available, or can be made, with colours, numbers or pictures.

Children need experience of written numbers. They may get this from books or wall posters. Help the under-5s to write numbers if they wish. Point out to them that there are two systems – letters for words, and numbers. Children may not have realised this.

The over-5s

Older children are learning more complicated ideas in maths, and are learning to write numbers correctly. They are coming to terms with the symbols for the basic mathematical operations of adding and subtracting. You will help the children if you are alert for some of the mistakes or worries that they may have. Some examples follow.

Sometimes children are overawed by larger numbers. They don't realise that numbers have to obey the same rules, however big they are. One and one makes two, but also one hundred and one hundred make two hundred; the same holds for thousands and millions.

Children may struggle with the different meaning of a number that is part of another number. For example, the written number '1' has different values in '145', '210' and '31'.

Children may have learned to read numbers up to 10 yet seem confused after that. They may not have realised that, in the Western system at least, numbers of 20 and above are read from left to right. Practice will help them to remember that the highest-value number comes first.

It is fine for 5- and 6-year-olds to continue to use their fingers to help them in counting. You can encourage 6- and 7-year-olds to try simple sums in their head – they can use their fingers or marks on paper when they get stuck. Explain to the children that if they practise, the point will come when they will know the answer.

Encourage children to say their workings out loud, when you are helping them. This will give you a hint of how much they understand.

Step in to help quickly if children announce that they are no good at maths. Help them see what they can do and try to identify the source of their confusion. Some children underestimate how much they have to practise before a number skill feels easier.

See computers and calculators as useful aids and make sure that you yourself are confident in working with either of them. If necessary, practise on the quiet! Make sure that girls and boys get equal access time on computers.

For your information

Unfortunately, some workers have uncomfortable memories of maths lessons from childhood. These can get in the way of their helping children.

There are some good books that can take the terror out of numbers; these also have many practical suggestions for activities. Try the following:
★ Graham, Alan 1983: *Help your Child with Maths* (Fontana).
★ Griffiths, Rose 1988: *Maths through Play* (MacDonald).
★ Usborne Parents' Guides: *Help your Child Learn Number Skills*.

Time

Some 7-year-olds may still be unsure about telling the time from a clock or watch; even 3- and 4-year-olds, though, can learn some sense of time. You can help through the following activities.

The routine
Chat with children about their home routine – what they do before they reach you in the morning or afternoon.

Children learn a lot by your having a routine during the day or half-day session that they are with you. They learn about which activity follows on from another. In this way children learn about a sequence in time.

For example, you might follow a pattern such as this. Activities at the beginning of the morning are followed by tidy-up time, then a story. After story-time, the morning children are collected to go home. The all-day children then get their cup, plate and cutlery and sit down for lunch. In your conversation you remind children of what is coming.

A weekly routine will help children learn the days of the week. Perhaps Monday is the day for telling about what happened at the weekend; Tuesday might be the day for a special music time; and so on.

How much time have we got?
The under-5s do not really understand exact measures of time like 'five minutes' or 'an hour'. Help them by using words about minutes or hours but expand this to explain that 'we have a very short time' or 'we have lots of time'.

Children are often fascinated by stopwatches, egg-timers and other kinds of timers. They may like to make improvised timers, for example using a bucket with a hole in the bottom which allows sand or water to trickle out into a bowl. Play games to explore how much children can do before the timer runs out. Can they button up their winter coat? Can they tidy up the bricks?

Children at ease with computers

Seasons and the passing of the year

Have a large wall calendar, one month to a page, and mark major events. Include individual celebrations like birthdays and celebrate the festivals of the major world religions. Remember that religious festivals do not always appear on the same date each year.

Children can paint and make displays about the seasons. You might have a board that can be changed each day to show the day, the month and the weather.

Past, present and future

Conversation with children is a very good way of helping them with both the words and the ideas involved in talking about now, times in the past and times into the future. Chat about trips you did together and what people did at the weekend. Plan together some of what you will all do tomorrow or next week.

You can introduce the idea of the historical past through books. Even 7-year-olds have only a hazy idea of history; you will realise this when you are asked questions such as 'Were you alive when the dinosaurs were around?'

Clock time

The under-5s are unlikely to be able to tell the time. They will probably first grasp the idea of times of the day, for example the time to leave home for the nursery, or lunchtime.

Remember that there are different ways of telling the time. Many clocks and watches still have moving hands, but some clocks and timers on equipment only have numbers. These digital systems may be 12- or 24-hour. Eventually children need to be able to understand all of these, but start with the one that is most familiar to them.

Help children link up familiar parts of their routine with the time on the clock. Have a clockface with moving hands or a board with numbers that you can make into digital time. Show them how the clock will look at lunchtime, going-home time or the time of their favourite television programme.

You may be working with 7-year-olds who have become confused. Be ready to use different material to help them, for example worksheets, a cardboard clock with moving hands, a real clock on the wall or watches. Make sure that the children are grasping the main things they should notice. With clock hands these are that there are hands of different sizes, and that there is a point where you change from 'past' one hour to 'to' the next hour. Children learning digital time need to realise which numbers tell the hour and which the minutes.

You might ask 7-year-olds and older to explain the rules of clock time in their own words. (You can do this as a game in which you are a visiting Martian.) This can help you and the child to focus positively on what she does understand and find out where that understanding breaks down.

Size

The measurement of size and different shapes is part of early mathematical ideas. Some of the books we have already suggested will help you here.

Children of 3 and 4 years often use the words 'big' and 'little' to cover height, weight and breadth. The same words are often used to describe age as well. You probably do this too, referring to the 'big' children in the group

Children learn to plan their work

Learning from sand play

or talking about things that may happen when an individual child is 'bigger'. Try to use the correct words as well as the more general 'big' or 'little'.

Children learn ideas of height and weight by comparing whether something or someone is taller or heavier. Then they can explore by creating their own means of measurement. For example, Tim may observe that Nicky is taller than him; Kathy may comment that the box of books is heavier than the toybox and she cannot lift the books. Here are just a few ideas.

- You can use height charts on the wall, noting how tall children are now and recording this for comparison in 6 months' time.
- Children can build brick towers or other constructions of different dimensions.
- You can use balances to see which item is heavier, or how many bricks it takes on one side to balance a book on the other side.

Children need to understand the idea of measuring before they are ready to understand centimetres and metres. Try an activity of measuring out a room or outdoor playspace by pacing. Use a standard measure like a length of string to compare the sizes of tables or the heights of brick towers.

Children confuse the size and shape of a container with how much it will hold. The idea of volume is difficult for the under-8s: you may demonstrate it by carefully using a standard measure. However, the under-5s appear to reject the evidence of their own eyes – 'He's got a bigger glass than me, of course he's got more squash!'

Through water play and other activities 6- and 7-year-olds grasp the concept that how much will go into something is related to overall how *large* the container is, not just how tall it is.

Shape

Children go through two stages in learning shapes – rather as with learning colours. First they have to see differences in shape around them, then they can begin to recognise particular shapes and learn the words to describe them.

You can choose play activities to help them learn. For example:

- sorting bricks into piles of different shapes;
- making shapes, with playdough or crafts like sewing;
- drawing round shapes or colouring them in;
- matching shapes in a Lotto game or shape dominoes;
- spotting shapes in the room, in pictures or furniture;
- identifying and naming cardboard or plastic shapes;
- posting shapes into a box with matching holes.

Notice in this last activity that it requires two skills: first the child has to recognise that a shape is the right one to fit a hole, then she has to turn the shape (in most cases) to align it with the hole. Children need a similar combination of skills to complete jigsaws, even simple ones.

Position and space

Different play activities can extend children's understanding of position and space. For example:

- Physical play and obstacle courses can help learning (crawling *under*, wriggling *through* or walking *behind*).
- Imaginative play with dolls and teddies or in the home corner can help learning about *in* and *on* (tucking dolls into bed, stirring make-believe food, and so on).
- Games like 'Simon says' can illustrate different movements, as can fun with music and movement (getting squashed together and then moving out to fingertip distance; stretching up and then out).

The under-5s are very unlikely to be able to tell left from right; it's a difficult idea to grasp. Even the over-5s are struggling with the apparent contradictions. For instance:

- 'My right hand is always the same hand; my left hand is always the same hand.'
- 'Now I can write, I put my pen into the same hand each time.'
- 'Yet when I am facing my friend in dance class and the teacher says "Turn to the right", we don't go the same way.'

Children are experiencing the problem of 'your right or my right?'

Many 5- and 6-year-olds distinguish left from right by getting clear about their writing hand, be this left or right; by elimination they work out the one remaining. With practice they become sure which is which. Some children have a mole or a scar on one hand which helps. Can you remember how *you* finally sorted out left from right?

Speed and distance

Children can become very confused about the concept of distance. In travelling, 'How far is it' becomes tied up with 'How long will it take us to get there?', which in turn depends on 'how fast' you are going – which depends on what form of transport you are using.

Don't expect the under-5s to become clear on this; you are helping them on their way. Use activities like these:

- physical play to explore moving fast and slow motion (again, music and movement can be an enjoyable medium);
- exploration of different kinds of transport and how fast they can travel;
- local trips to give children an idea about relative distances and times taken.

Check whether they can remember the route to the local market or the park. Use a timer or help them read the time to check on how long the whole trip has taken. If you are using buses or trains for a trip, involve children in planning how to make the journey.

Use or make simplified maps with the children. The over-5s will become interested in maps or globes showing the countries of the world.

Mark towns or other countries where they have friends or relatives. Link books or television programmes to places on your map.

How things work

Ideas of describing and measuring are part of understanding how the world works. Another part is literally what makes things happen. Children can be fascinated by this and by 4 or 5 years of age can ask you questions that really make you think.

Young children begin to observe the events that are explained by scientific principles, without yet being able to grasp the 'why' to explain the 'what'. Many of the play activities suggested earlier in this section and in section 4.2 are also a possible route to illustrating basic principles of how the world works. For example:

- *Water play* is also a way to explore floating and sinking, or how some substances change if you soak them.
- *Cooking* is a kind of chemistry. You can show what happens with differences in temperature; when you mix solids with water; and how to bring about changes – for example, beating cream to make it thick.
- *Music* and the making of instruments demonstrate the science of making sounds and how sound travels.
- *Crafts* such as kite-making show the principles of flight and may illustrate the influence of the weather.
- *Trips out* can be a way to help children observe plants and wildlife. You do not have to live in the countryside – some city parks are full of things to watch.
- *Growing* flowers or vegetables can be an enjoyable project. Children will learn that they cannot keep pulling plants up to see what they are doing! Mustard and cress or carrot tops grow quite quickly.

For your information

You will find many books to extend your ideas.
★ For the younger children, try the 'Threads' series from A & C Black. Usborne has a number of books with ideas adaptable for supervised activities for children as young as 3.
★ 6- and 7-year olds might manage some experiments with less supervision, for example the 'First Science' series (Usborne). For investigating the natural world, try the 'Eyewitness Explorer' series from Dorling Kindersley.

6.3 How you can help – ideas about people and growing up

The under-8s will be learning about all of the following:

- how people differ in looks, which includes differences of race and sex;
- relationships between people, including how families work;
- how people behave and rules for behaviour;
- babies and being born;
- getting older, illness and death.

You do not, of course, have to sort out all these ideas with the under-8s, just be aware that they will be developing their ideas and beliefs and help them. You can do this in a number of ways.

Chatting and looking

Children are often curious about other people. Young children are uninhibited about staring. When they have learned to talk they make comments on what they notice, and often ask personal questions loudly in public places. Try to satisfy their curiosity as well as teaching children how they can ask personal questions more discreetly.

If you welcome conversation with children, you will be able to correct factual misunderstandings. You can also gently challenge prejudices without making children feel got at.

Sometimes the questions just keep coming . . .

Books and projects

You will find that one leads to another. Children get interested in a book, or they ask you questions and you start a project with them. Or else you have the idea for a project or a display and the children get interested enough to want to pore over some books.

You may be able to extend some projects by inviting in parents or local people to talk briefly about a relevant topic of which they have experience.

Families round the world

As you listen to children you will hear them struggling to follow the idea that one person can be in different relationships. In the end a 7-year-old is coming to an understanding that 'Daddy is my father, but he is also Grandma's son, Mummy's husband and Uncle Darren's brother'.

It can be even more difficult for children to apply this idea to themselves. In a two-child family, a 4-year-old girl may well say, 'Yes, I have a brother called Paresh.' Asked if Paresh has a sister, she may say 'No'.

Source material on families

Many children will experience a family life that changes. You will be able to get books to illustrate different family set-ups: examples are the 'Friends' series and Sue Wagstaff's *Wayne is Adopted* (both from A & C Black) and Priscilla Galloway's *Jennifer has Two Daddies* (The Women's Press). There are more suggestions in VOLCUF's booklet, *Changing Families*.

Many of the books suggested throughout this workbook are good illustrations of everyday life for children and adults. Children are interested in families and ways of life that are both within and outside their experience.

There are suggestions for good books and series in sections 3.4 and 5.2. You could also try the 'Beans' series (A & C Black) or the 'Focus On' series (Hamish Hamilton) for a round-the-world perspective. ACER and VOLCUF (see Appendix 2 for addresses) have good posters of children. Sometimes you will be able to cut out useful photographs from magazines like *Nursery World* or *Child Education*. Galt sell jigsaws in the 'Just Like Us' and 'Children of the World' series.

Feelings

Children are beginning to understand feelings, both their own and other people's. They need to talk about emotions and you can support those conversations by books. Two possible series are Janine Amos's *Feelings* (Cherrytree Books) or ACER's *Myself* (address in Appendix 2).

Sometimes children faced with an upsetting event, such as losing a loved grandparent or the divorce of their parents, can be helped by reading about a fictional character in a similar situation. A book does not do all the work, of course; children need the opportunity to talk and be reassured if appropriate. (See also sections 3.5 and 7.2.)

When I grow up, I might be . . .

Growing up

Children often enjoy projects that illustrate family history or the development from their own babyhood to their current age. They may like to bring in photographs. Some children will be surprised to realise that you too were once a baby.

Although 4- and 5-year-olds will have realised that there are boys, girls, men and women, it may be a year or so before they understand the links. Boys inevitably become men and may become fathers. Girls grow into women, who may become mothers.

Before the end of the week, Fudge asked the big question. 'How did the baby get inside you, Mommy?' So Mom borrowed my copy of *How Babies Are Made*, and she read it to Fudge. As soon as he had the facts straight, he was telling anybody and everybody exactly how Mom and Dad had made their baby. . . . He told the girl on the till at the supermarket. Her eyes got bigger and bigger until Mom said, 'That's enough, Fudgie.' 'But I'm getting to the good part,' Fudge said.

From Judy Blume's *Superfudge*, p. 14 (Piper Books, 1980).

Some young children may have been taught at home that boys and girls should have different toys or play different games; they may have learned that one sex is more important than the other. Parents need to understand that you will be challenging any remarks or behaviour that imply this. You need also to make clear that you will be encouraging all the children to try the full range of play.

You particularly need to understand parents' opinions about how conversations about birth and death should be handled. Families may have strongly held beliefs about how much and in what way children should be told about these topics. Religious beliefs will enter into how they explain death to their children.

For your information

★ We suggest some good series of books in section 3.5. Clare Rayner has also written two books suitable for the under-8s: *The Body Book* (1978) and *The Getting Better Book* (1985). Both are published by Piccolo.

Religious beliefs

There may be a number of religious beliefs represented by the families with whom you have contact. Be honest about your own views as well as showing respect for the different faiths of others.

You may work in a nursery or group which is aligned with a particular religious belief. You are still responsible under the Children Act 1989 for helping children to understand and respect beliefs other than their own.

You may need to extend your own knowledge of the major faiths of the world. As we reminded you in section 3.2, about religious belief and diet, most of the world's major faiths have different sects: within any religion, families will vary in how strictly they apply particular beliefs in everyday life.

You are aiming for a friendly working relationship with parents. You are fortunate if you live in an area in which several religions are practised, since this may provide more opportunities for information and advice from parents. Some of the books we suggest for children will help you too, especially if you do not have parents or fellow workers with a broad knowledge of more than one religion.

You can celebrate some of the major religious festivals of world faiths. This is respectful when children in your group belong to a range of different faiths; it is also a way to teach children a little about different religions.

Keep it simple but make sure that what you say is correct. Don't explain a festival in one religion in terms of another religion. For example, Eid-ul-Fitr (Muslim), Diwali (Hindu and Sikh) and Christmas (Christian) all involve the giving of gifts. This does not make Diwali a kind of Christmas, or vice versa.

Celebrating festivals, like Chinese New Year, can be great fun. However, don't forget that there are serious messages within the lively events.

Don't drag any of the celebrations out long beyond the appropriate dates. Children get fed up if they seem to be spending weeks making decorations and wall displays.

For your information

Books for children that you will also find informative:
★ The 'Seasonal Festivals' and 'Religious Stories' series published by Wayland.
★ The 'Our Culture' and 'My Belief' series published by Franklin Watts.
★ Angela Wood 1990: *Faith Stories for Today* (BBC/Longman).

Nottingham Educational Supplies publish pre-school festival packs which combine some information with suggestions of activities.
★ Contact them at: Ludlow Hill Road, West Bridgford, Nottingham NG2 6HD (*tel.* 0602 234251).

7 Children's behaviour and adults' behaviour

7.1 Why do children behave as they do?

You may sometimes feel very confused over the reasons for a child's behaviour. 'Why did she do that?' you ask yourself, and anybody else who will listen.

You probably only ask this question when a child is misbehaving. You may be pleasantly surprised when a child is unexpectedly co-operative, but you probably don't spend as much time thinking or talking about this stroke of good fortune. This is a pity, since you can learn as much from children who are behaving well as from agonising over those who are driving you up the wall.

Do remember that likely reasons for children's behaviour may not immediately make sense from an adult point of view. You need to be ready to look through children's eyes.

Be ready also to look at how *you* are behaving and how you could be affecting the total situation. The children aren't the only people present.

Most likely there are several reasons which could explain any child's behaviour at any one time. Children's behaviour is influenced by any of the following.

Children copy other children and adults

Even very young children watch and imitate the behaviour of others – you will be delighted by some of the actions that they learn from copying. Children may learn new ways of playing from their friends. Similarly, they may be more willing to go happily to the toilet because they see other children who go without making a fuss.

However, children may also copy undesirable behaviour – hitting another child to get a favourite toy, or repeating swear words or aggressive language.

Children do what they are told to do

As well as copying others' behaviour, children also learn rules for behaviour which they are told by adults or other children.

You may be very frustrated at the times when children don't do what you have asked; at other times they will follow your requests. Gradually they can learn to keep to realistic boundaries that you set. (There is more about rules in section 7.3.)

They also follow suggestions from other children. Perhaps a child joins in with an activity because a friend has proposed it. The over-5s in particular are becoming aware of the rules determined by other children, which may be very different from the adults' rules.

Children learn to take turns

Children have strong feelings and emotional needs

Children's feelings affect their behaviour but this works in different ways.

Sometimes children just *want* to do something. They see the biscuits, they know that they have eaten up to their limit but they fail to resist sneaking another one. They are tempted beyond their ability to resist.

Just like adults, children sometimes react to unhappy or angry feelings by lashing out in words or actions at someone else.

Children have emotional needs for affection, attention and for a sense of being special in some way. They do not necessarily seek to meet these needs in ways that are acceptable to adults, but they do tend to persist in behaviour that – from their point of view – seems to be effective.

For example, you may be at your wits' end trying to deal with a child who argues incessantly with you in front of the group. This child may continue behaving like this so long as you rise to the bait: she is thrilled with the sense of self-importance she feels by clashing with you in front of the audience of her peers.

Children draw conclusions from their own observations

Different adults behave differently

Children learn from their experience with different adults. Consequently, they may behave differently depending on who is in charge of them. Younger children are unlikely to express their deductions in words but you can guess these from their behaviour. However, 5- or 6-year-olds and older may confide in you – 'Grandad is a softy. I can get anything out of him.'

Children may learn to behave co-operatively when they are in the care of one adult. They do not necessarily behave this way with every other adult who has charge of them. For example, 3-year-old Craig has learned to scream for sweets by the supermarket checkout. His mother is very embarrassed by this behaviour. She refuses him sweets several times but then always gives way. However, when his childminder is in charge she continues to say 'No'. She is willing to walk Craig firmly away, still screaming. Craig tries the screaming trick once or twice more with his minder and then gives up. With his mother, though, he continues to pester for sweets at the checkout.

Words and actions

Young children will notice contradictions between what adults say and what then happens. Older children may comment in words that adults are not being fair.

For example, young children are unlikely to meet your request that they wait their turn for toys in short supply unless you make sure that their waiting pays off. Suppose that some children aggressively jump the queue: children who would have been co-operative in turn-taking will either start to push and shove or will become distressed. (Sections 7.3 and 7.4 have more about consequences of actions and what children learn.)

Children don't always foresee the consequences of their actions

Younger children don't always understand what might happen, and this can get them into trouble. For example, you might find 4-year-old Emily in a puddle of water: she was trying to help by emptying a bowl of water, but it was too heavy for her and she lost control.

She's not sure of your reaction here

7.2 Making sense of what is going on

Child-watching

You can learn a great deal from watching children. Look for patterns. Sometimes one event may trigger another in a fairly simple way; often, though, the pattern is more complicated. (You may like to look as well at section 2.7, on observation.)

In a busy working life with children you may be tempted to focus on just one bit of the total action, and often this is a child's behaviour. However, a sequence of events leads up to and away from anything that a child or adult does: try to make the effort to look for patterns in what happens. You may well gain a broader perspective that will help you encourage the kind of behaviour you would rather have from children.

IT'S MORE FUN EATING ON THE STREET WHEN THEY TELL ME NOT TO.

Learning how to get attention

Children have sometimes learned ways of behaving that successfully get your attention through actions that you do not want to encourage. From some children's point of view, it won't matter that they are being told off: they still have your attention. They don't then have any good reason – any motivation – to behave differently.

It can help a frustrating situation to focus on what you can do and try the following:

- *Explain what you would like*   Explain simply to a child how you would rather she attracted your attention when you are working with a group.

- *Reward preferred behaviour*   Try to give her more attention and more promptly when she talks to you quietly. Thank her when she waits, even for a moment.

- *Initiate friendly contact*   Pay the child some friendly attention on occasions when she has not demanded it.

Avoiding battles

There may be children in your care with whom you seem to be arguing several times every day. When you think about incidents afterwards, you realise that you have often fought over trivial matters. It dawns on you that thoughts go through your mind like, 'Who does he think is!' or 'She isn't going to get away with this!' Some children successfully provoke you into power battles which they enjoy and which leave you worn out.

There are possible changes that you could make in how you behave towards children who love a dramatic battle.

- *Don't argue unnecessarily*   Be clear in your own mind about rules on which you must stand firm. Don't enter a power battle with children over something that does not really matter. Your pride is not sufficient reason to fight – find a way to turn away with your dignity intact.

- *Seek privacy, and respect the child*   If you judge that you do have to argue something out with a child, try to do this without an audience of the other children. Do your very best to stay calm and resist any temptation to belittle the child.

EXAMPLE

Melanie is 4 years old. She has not learned quiet ways to attract adults' attention: she shouts and screams for help with any activity. At story time, Melanie pokes the other children. She is so persistent that her shouts and tugging at adult sleeves often get attention more effectively than children who touch an arm for attention or ask for help at normal volume. Story time is punctuated with workers telling Melanie off.

1   Are you working with a child like Melanie?
2   Are you and colleagues getting very irritated although you realise that this doesn't help?
3   Have you found ways of behaving that have encouraged a child like Melanie to try less disruptive ways of getting attention?

- *Affirm the child's contributions* Ask for her opinion before she shouts it out. (Do this for other children as well, of course.) Perhaps a child contradicts you but you realise that he has the basis of a good idea. Agree with him and present it to the group as an alternative that they can choose if they wish. Thank him for the idea. Ignore the fact that he could have expressed it more politely.

- *Offer responsibility* Look for ways to give children responsibilities and opportunities for them to lead in a constructive way.

EXAMPLE

Sam, who is 5, relishes an argument. Whenever an adult tells him off or suggests that he tries a piece of work again, he argues loudly. When a worker gives an instruction to the whole group, Sam whispers to his neighbour and grins, looking to see how the worker reacts.

Workers find themselves in regular conflict with Sam, insisting that he do things like pick up every last pencil or apologise for every cheeky remark. They find themselves unable to ignore him. Other children appear to look up to

Sam, yet he is not the kind of group leader that any adult wants to encourage.

1 Are you working with some children who always want the last word?
2 Be honest with yourself: does your pride get in the way of a calm way of handling the confrontations?
3 How can you constructively use the child's qualities of leadership?

You may find that you look for patterns more often when a child's behaviour is *un*acceptable to you. Please don't think of child-watching, or the talking with children which follows, as ways to track down who is to blame: this kind of fault-finding is rarely constructive in work with children.

Observing individual children

You may find it useful to gather more details if you are very frustrated in your attempts to deal with a particular child. For general issues about observation, look at section 2.7.

Look carefully at what the child is doing

You need to get beyond any shorthand that you have been using. Perhaps you and fellow workers describe a 4-year-old boy as 'aggressive'. But what exactly do you mean by the word? Does he bite other children or you? Does he use words to make other children cry? Does he hit or slap without any warning?

How do you usually deal with biting or hitting?

You cannot stand outside yourself and observe yourself, so you need to think this over in a quiet moment. You could also, of course, observe how other workers tend to deal with the behaviour.

Are there some ways of handling incidents that seem to be more successful? Can you see it coming sometimes? Are you using opportunities to step in before this child hits out?

How do you want this child to behave?

You and your fellow workers are probably very clear about what you want

This is a game – at the moment!

this child to stop doing. Are you equally clear about how you would *rather* he dealt with the situations that seem to provoke his behaviour?

Consider your notes after observing this child for a week or so. Think over the times when this child bit or hit. How could he have reacted differently? Do you want him to be more patient in waiting? Would you rather he used words than his fists? Do you want him to come to tell you about problems with other children?

Are you encouraging the behaviour that you want?

Watch what happens if this child does react differently. Is he praised, thanked or given a cuddle?

Can you take the chance when you are close by to help this child to wait for a toy or to back off from a confrontation with another child?

Be alert to any discouraging reactions from adults – you or your fellow workers. You may not mean to be unkind, but comments such as 'Well, it makes a change not having to tell you off' or 'How long are you going to keep that up?' reinforce the child's sense of being seen as a problem.

Talking with children

This part of the workbook has emphasised the importance of what you do with children. Part of what you can do, of course, is talk with children.

Some of the suggestions for positive consequences in section 7.3 are in terms of what you say. You may experience more problems in talking with children when they have misbehaved or when you are puzzled about what is going on.

Be straight with children

Be honest and straightforward with a child who has misbehaved. Say, for example, 'I'm cross that you slapped Jerome. I don't want you to do that.' Children tend not to react well to unclear criticism and emotional pressure, as in comments such as 'Don't you think that was a nasty thing to do?' They are at risk of being in the wrong however they answer. Remember what it was like when you were a child: if you *agreed* with the angry adult, then you had admitted that you knowingly did something nasty; if you *disagreed*, adults tended to get even crosser – *they* clearly thought your behaviour was nasty, otherwise why on earth were they going on about it?

Don't insist on good enough reasons

Children have reasons for what they do when they misbehave, though these may be hard to uncover. If you succeed in understanding the reasons, you will often disagree with the children's view that these reasons justify this behaviour.

If you ask children 'Why?' when they have misbehaved, you will rarely get an answer you like. You will almost certainly ask in an accusing and cross tone of voice. The most you will get is a justification that starts with 'because' and probably includes some variation of 'she started it'. It is better to try to remain calm and to ask a more open question, such as 'What happened?' or 'Tell me about it'.

Listen to what children tell you. Sort out what you can and disagree if need be, but show the children that you have listened properly to their point of view.

Chatting with children about a persistent problem

Take the opportunity of a quieter time to talk with a child about difficulties. Make it clear that you are chatting together about a problem and looking for ways to help: you are not just getting at them. This is equally true if you have a small-group discussion with 6- or 7-year-olds.

Bear in mind the following guidelines.

- *Keep it simple*   Keep your words simple and your sentences short.
- *Listen respectfully*   Talking should be an exchange in which you *listen* at least as much as you speak. If children cannot get their views heard then you are talking *at* them. They will think you are nagging, and they'll be right.
- *Be willing to stop*   Don't continue conversations beyond the point where the child is willing to talk.
- *Check that you have understood*   Make sure that you understand what the child is communicating to you. Put it back in your own words and ask if you have got the message. Do this also in a group discussion with children.
- *Encourage children to check that they have understood*   Ask children to put your main message into their own words. Give them a chance to ask any questions.
- *Let them be themselves*   Don't pressurise children to agree with you. Be grateful if, on occasion, they follow what you ask them to do.

7.3 Clear rules and consequences

Rules – making and applying them

Young and older children will often keep to a short set of realistic rules. They like to please adults who do not ask too much and who give in return. However, remember that *your* rules aren't the only set in existence.

Children can put pressure on each other. They may dare each other to do something that one or both children know is not allowed. This is a greater risk with the over-5s.

Some children bring rules from home that you do not welcome. For example, you may be insisting that children *tell* you if they are in dispute: a child may inform you, however, that 'My Mum says I'm allowed to hit people.'

Children deserve rules that are clear. They should be applied fairly and communicated with a warmth that shows you care about the children.

Rules are much more likely to work if you follow these guidelines.

Be clear in your own mind about your rules

It may help to make a short list for yourself. The rules should be realistic. Allow for where you are working and the age or ability of the children.

The list should be short and you may decide to put it on the wall. Try to have some illustrations as well as written words.

Explain the rules to the children

You need to explain each rule and your reasons. Explain simply what happens if the rule gets broken. How are you going to reward children who obey the rules?

Children can sort some things out for themselves

Children deserve the reasons for a rule, although the under-3s may not always understand. Be prepared that the over-5s may challenge your reasons.

Rules are better stated positively. You are wiser to say 'I want you to keep the sand in the sand tray' than 'You're not to drop sand on the floor.'

Apply any rules consistently

There is no point in having a rule if it is not applied. You must be consistent in your own behaviour and a group of workers must support each other. If there are disagreements amongst the adults, sort them out away from the children.

Obey your own rules. If the children aren't allowed to eat sweets, don't eat sweets yourself in front of them. If an after-school club has a system of forfeits for swearing, you must submit as well.

Remind children of the rules

Be patient, you will have to repeat yourself many times. The over-5s may be reminded by posters such as 'Put your litter in here' or 'Don't run'. However, you may have to change the posters from time to time. Children will stop noticing any poster that becomes part of the wallpaper.

Review your rules from time to time

You can involve the over-5s in this review. Small groups of over-5s may be responsive to general chats about rules and the reasons. Be ready to listen to children's opinions about whether a rule is working.

Be clear about how rules work

The rules which affect how a group room or a classroom or a family home is run are not always absolute. However, children need to know the amount of 'give' in a rule. Some adults run a 'red, yellow and green' system. (The idea comes from traffic lights.)

A red rule is an absolute 'no': it is always enforced. For example, neither adults nor children are allowed to hit children; offensive racist or sexist terms are never allowed. Children or adults who break the red rules are *always* picked up on it.

A yellow rule has some variation around a consistent theme. An example might be that children are not usually allowed sweets. An exception may be at a birthday party or on some other special occasion.

A green rule is an absolute 'yes'. For example, children are allowed to ask to go to the toilet whenever they wish; there is no 'You should have gone earlier, you'll have to wait'.

Can you let children get away with anything?

You may decide sometimes to ignore minor infringements of rules, for example if you suspect a child wants to stir things up. However, without some other distraction children tend to persist until they get a reaction.

If you stress that a rule is very important, then you really must enforce it. So, think carefully before you say this.

Offensive remarks

Children will be rude to each other from time to time. Sometimes you may decide to ignore an incident or let the children sort it out for themselves.

Posters can sometimes act as reminders to older children

However, you should not ignore patterns of insult based on prejudice, such as racist or sexist taunts, or verbal attacks on a child who is disabled.

Children and prejudice

Young children notice racial differences. Especially in a racially mixed community, children as young as 3 will be aware of differences in skin colour. It would be very surprising if children did not notice, since they are very alert to the world around them.

However, racial prejudice, like any other kind of prejudice, does not follow inevitably from noticing differences between people. Children may or may not comment immediately on racial differences that they see. Children who have not learned prejudice may see no reason to comment on what is to them just one more way in which their friends or other people differ in looks. Some children, even though they have learned a racist outlook, do not make racist comments until a particular situation arises.

Reading on . . .

★ There is an English saying, 'Sticks and stones may break my bones but words will never hurt me.' Unfortunately this is not true. A study of school-age children highlighted how deeply hurt children can be by what is said. This is reported by Barry Troyna and Richard Hatcher in *Racism in Children's Lives: a study of mainly white primary schools* (Routledge/ National Children's Bureau, 1992).

Steps to dealing with offensive remarks

You need to support any child whose feelings have been hurt. You may sometimes suggest that the child ignores what has been said. Show the child that you recognise her feelings, however, and that you take her seriously.

Make it clear to all the children that there are some words that you absolutely will not have used in your group. These should include racist or sexist terms of abuse and using a child's disability as an insult. This point needs careful handling: it is not fair if children who are distressed by rude remarks about their mother or about the size of their nose feel that they don't get a sympathetic hearing unless the remarks are also racist.

When you feel you should reprimand a child who has been hurtful to another, make it brief. It is probably better also to make your comments in private, as he is less likely then to feel humiliated and strike back at the same or another child. Communicate to such children that you still like them; it is just that you object to what they have said.

The child who has made the offensive remark may claim that it is 'just a joke'. You need to communicate that a joke, or 'a bit of fun', is something that both parties enjoy. If one child is distressed, then this cannot be a joke.

Suppose there is a spate of offensive remarks. These may focus on one child and victimise him in this way. Or else certain children may be targeted, perhaps in a racist way. You may want to tackle this as a topic. The ways you choose will depend on the children's age. Older children may be able to talk about the issues; younger children may need a story that illustrates how all children feel if someone attacks them as individuals.

It is important that everyone in a staff team consistently takes the same approach. Part of your early contact with parents should include an explanation of the values of your group or centre and how you handle children's behaviour.

Positive and negative consequences

It matters how you behave with children. They are keen observers of your behaviour and they will change in response to how you behave. Your options really fall into two categories – positive and negative consequences that follow on from what children do.

Always be ready to look at what is going on from the children's standpoint. Ask yourself: if I were a child, would I feel that it was worth behaving well?

Sometimes workers, and parents too, put most energy into spotting wrongdoing and devising punishments for those who break rules. This can have a rather depressing effect on you, and it is very discouraging for children.

Think about your own work as an adult. Have you sometimes felt that you would appreciate a few more compliments? Have you had jobs where the only way you could deduce that somebody thought you were working well was when they didn't nag you? Children are not so different in their feelings.

Positive consequences

You have a range of choices here. Children appreciate a selection from the following.

Say 'Thank you'

Thank her for her help in laying the table. Tell him that you appreciate his patience in waiting until you had finished changing the baby.

You can communicate 'Thank you' by words and a smile. Some children will welcome a hug or a touch on the hand or shoulder.

Say 'Well done'

Encourage a child by noticing that he has finished his construction. Show that you recognise that she persevered, although she found buttoning up her coat so difficult.

Reward with your praise

Admire what children have done and how they have done it. You will find that families vary in how much they use praise; some are concerned that this is tantamount to spoiling children and will give them a swelled head. There seem to be both family and cultural traditions in the use of praise.

Explain to parents how you work and reassure them, if necessary, that your compliments to children are not a sign that you let them get away with things.

Special rewards

There is nothing the matter with special rewards so long as you do not let them get out of hand. Children who have been very well behaved do not have to be rewarded with sweets. Instead, you may for example be able to arrange a special activity.

The over-5s often appreciate symbols such as stars and stickers. They may like certificates, for example for punctuality or especially hard work.

There comes a point when children prefer a private word of thanks and may be embarrassed by very public symbols of recognition. You may not encounter this since it is more likely to become an issue with 9- and 10-year-olds, but watch out for the 6- or 7-year-old who seems uncomfortable with public praise. Ask him if he would rather you spoke with him on the quiet.

Negative consequences

Some of what you will do in response to what a child does will be negative. By negative we do not mean bad; we mean the opposite of positive.

When you use negative consequences, you don't have to be thoroughly unpleasant, in fact it's better if you are not. However, you do have to be firm and consistent. Any negative consequences should be clearly linked to what a child has done; they should follow on very close in time to when the child has done whatever it is. They should be brief and should not be dragged out over the day.

If at all possible you should warn a child what will happen if he persists in behaving in a certain way. Give him a chance to change. If he carries on, then apply any negative consequences consistently. Your behaviour should not vary according to your mood. The children will not know where they stand with you if you are unpredictable.

You have a number of options.

The warning look
This can work well with young and older children so long as they know from experience that you follow this up. You may have warning gestures, look with a 'beady eye' or give other messages through body language. (Look at section 5.1 to remind yourself that some gestures do not have the same meaning worldwide.)

Telling a child firmly not to do something
You can restate a rule with firm words and body language. If this is a 'don't' message, you will help young children if you immediately offer a 'do'. This is best accompanied by moving them away from the source of temptation or trouble. Give them something to do which distracts their attention.

Ignore what the child is doing
Sometimes the best negative consequence is to ignore what a child is doing. (One example is the description of Sam in section 7.2.) But it is important that you do not set about ignoring the child in a wider sense: you are simply choosing to ignore specific behaviour.

Removals
Especially with young children, it is sometimes best to remove a child from another child, an activity or a toy. You should do this as calmly as you can. Get both children involved in some other activity. Explain to a child removed from a toy how she needs to behave if she wants it back; keep this explanation very simple.

Children sometimes need to cool off. You may tell a child firmly to 'Sit on that chair and be quiet for a while.' This 'while' should not be long – a few minutes at most. You need to return to the child, perhaps have a brief chat (see 'Talking with children' in section 7.2), and get him settled back into an activity.

Cooling-off periods do not work if sitting on a particular chair leads to teasing remarks from other children. Nor do they work if children are left for what seems to them a very long time or if they are forgotten.

Telling another adult

A possible negative consequence is to inform a child that someone else will be told about their bad behaviour. This may be the head of centre or school or the child's parent.

Some children care deeply about this and do not want it to happen. Others, however, don't care a jot: you can still consider using telling as a negative consequence, but accept that the results may be unpredictable. When you choose to talk with a parent, offer the child the chance to tell first.

Making restitution

This is a good example of our point that negative consequences are not inevitably awful. Given a choice, children would probably not clear up a mess they had made or apologise to a child they had hurt. However, you can insist on these consequences and carry them through in a constructive way.

Children who clear up a mess without a big fuss deserve thanks, even though they should not have caused it in the first place.

There are a number of positive and negative consequences that you would be unwise to use, either because they do not work or because it is unfair to children. Section 7.4 covers tactics to avoid.

Reading on . . .

★ Laishley, Jennie 1987: *Working with Young Children*, Part Three (Hodder & Stoughton).
★ Pearce, John 1989: *Fighting, Teasing and Bullying*; *Tantrums and Tempers*; *Worries and Fears*; *Bad Behaviour* (Thorsons).

For work with school-age groups try:
★ Elliott, Michele 1991: *Bullying – a practical guide to coping for schools* (Longman with Kidscape).
★ Fontana, David 1985: *Classroom Control* (BPS/Methuen).

7.4 Tactics to avoid

It is hard working with children. There will be times when your patience runs very thin indeed. You may look back on a day and realise that you have not handled a situation as well as you might – perhaps you will be thinking over how you usually handle trying times with a particular child, or chatting with a fellow worker.

Be ready to recognise if you are using some of these unhelpful tactics. With each of the following suggestions for you to avoid, there are ideas of more constructive ways to behave.

Some people do judge boys' and girls' behaviour differently

Nagging

This behaviour comes in two basic versions.

Complaining and moaning about children

You shouldn't indulge in moaning about the children in front of them – *you* would think it very rude if they did this to you. If you are having trouble with a child, you may find help in talking it over with a fellow worker. However, your aim is to find some positive action as well as to unload your frustrations.

If a child has misbehaved, then you should deal with it. The incident is then over. It's not fair to keep harking back to it later.

Repeating yourself, perhaps many times

Sooner or later, you will be tempted by this tactic. Perhaps, you think, children who take no notice the first time will be more likely to do what you say if you say it again and again. Unfortunately, though, the opposite is usually true: children stop listening to you or become resentful because they feel got at.

Try very hard to follow a more positive pattern:

- *Get close to the child*   Don't shout from a distance.
- *Make sure you have his attention*   Say his name or touch him before you say any more.
- *Tell him once clearly what you want*   Show him as well as using words.
- *Watch him to see whether he does as you have asked*   Give him help if he needs it.
- *Thank him* if he has followed what you said.
- *If he hasn't done as he was told, tell him again calmly*   Ask him to tell you in his own words what he thinks you want him to do. Correct any misunderstandings.
- *Stand by and make sure that he does do what you have asked*   Then thank him.

ACTIVITY

1   Watch a child whom you think of as a nuisance. Try to be more aware of your pattern of behaviour with him.

- Do you tend to tell him off when you might let another child get away with a warning look?
- Do you tell him to do something several times, scarcely waiting to see whether he is going to do it?

2   Try the suggestions in the text.

Shouting

There will be occasions when you need to raise your voice. If children are doing something dangerous, they must be warned quickly. However, watch out for the habit of shouting. If you shout a great deal, the children will raise their voices. Then you shout louder and everybody has a headache at the end of the day.

Shouting as a regular habit has the same disadvantage as nagging – the children stop listening to you.

- *Shout only the few words that you need to get a child's attention, perhaps just her name*   Then go closer to her or beckon her to you and continue with what you want to say.
- *Practise making your voice carry without raising the volume to high levels*   If you're a man, you have an advantage because your voice is pitched lower. If you're a woman, don't get despondent: try to hold your voice lower in your throat and use an emphasis on the words.
- *Don't shout at children who shout*   Ask them quietly to say it again in a normal voice.
- *You can try whispering games*   This may be especially helpful if a group has become very noisy by habit.
- *Use a signal*   Decide on a gesture you will use for 'Quiet now' or use one or two loud handclaps.

Endless rewards and empty threats

Your aim is that children behave fairly well for most of the time because they want to. Avoid creating a situation in which children only behave if you promise endless treats. You're trying to make life more enjoyable if children behave with consideration for others. You don't want to have to pay them for it.

If you behave towards children in a way that is kind and fair, they will almost certainly want to please you. If you show that you expect well of them, they are far more likely to behave well, even if they drive other people to distraction.

There is no point in making threats that you are unable or would be unwilling to carry out. Sometimes, fraught adults do threaten something dire and regret it afterwards. Children will appreciate a measured change of mind – 'I've thought about what I said. I don't think I was being fair. What I am going to do is this.' However, you can't afford to do this too often or be seen to be swayed easily by ferocious nagging from children. It's better to avoid empty threats at the outset.

Ridiculing children

Don't resort to trying to make children look silly in front of their peers, even though you may be tempted when a child is very rude or constantly challenges you.

Humiliating children is an unfair tactic and it will almost certainly rebound on you. For one thing, the child whom you have ridiculed may pay you back in some way. For another, the other children will lose respect for you; they will be less likely to trust you, thinking that if you do this to one child you might do it to anyone.

If children need reprimanding, speak directly to them about their behaviour. Avoid an interested audience of other children if you can.

Labelling children

It is very important that you keep a child's *behaviour* separate from him or her as an individual. This is as true for children who are well behaved as for those who are not. Each child should feel confident that you like her or him, regardless of what they do. They should not fear that your feelings for them as individuals change with the moment.

Sometimes you will be cross with children, and for good reason. Make sure they know that, cross as you are, this doesn't touch your care for each of them as a person. It is what they are *doing* that is the focus of your anger. They can change how they behave.

In calmer times be prepared to say this clearly in words. Even 4-year-olds can follow the message of 'I like you. I don't like it when you slap Andreas.' You can explain that your anger and your caring for them are on two quite different tracks: bad behaviour is just that, it doesn't make a bad child. To make this believable to any child, you must avoid such threats as 'I don't like you any more' or 'I won't like you if you keep doing that'.

Do monitor the children and other adults – staff or parents – for any tendency to label a child. The so-called 'bad' or 'naughty' child can end up being blamed when something was not her fault. She may even get blamed when she was not actually in the room when the wrongdoing occurred.

Taking a dislike to a child

Some workers with young children will deny that they ever dislike children in their care, but it does happen. Even if this child is behaving in a way that would drive anyone mad, you must not allow your dislike to make things worse. The following may help.

Admit to yourself how you feel
It may not make you feel good about yourself, but it is real. Consider talking your feelings over with a colleague. Don't tell the child. This is *your* problem and *you* must resolve it as soon as you can.

Are you under a lot of stress at work or home?

Your frustrations with this child may be the last straw. Her behaviour may not be so very different from a few months ago, but perhaps *you* feel less able to deal with it.

What are you expecting of this child? Are you being fair?

For example, are you focusing so much on Neil's appalling table manners that you don't notice his careful drawings? Morag's behaviour is very disruptive in the group, but have you considered that she may be bored? Perhaps she needs more challenge.

Search out some positives

If you only notice when children are behaving badly then most of what you say to them is nagging. You become less and less able to see a positive side and the children may give up trying because you are too hard to please.

If she is doing something that needs to be dealt with, say it once – not a dozen times. Wait until you have given her a chance to be right. Put your energy onto finding things to like and admire about her.

It may help to make a list for yourself. On one side of the paper you can write down all you want about 'I am irritated when Morag does this . . .'. Then, for every item on this side, you must write something positive on the other side that starts with 'I am pleased when Morag does this . . .'. Or you might write 'What I admire about Morag is . . .'.

Concentrate on the positives and compliment her every time the opportunity arises. Then you have a chance of improving your relationship with her.

Punishing a whole group

The tactic of punishing everyone for the bad behaviour of a few is more common with workers responsible for the over-5s. Children are adamant that it is not fair.

Sometimes you may be forced to cancel an activity for a whole group because you cannot trust one or two children to behave themselves. Try to offer something special to the well-behaved children.

Do your best to avoid this by leaving the untrustworthy ones with another worker. Explain your reason to the children concerned and spell out clearly how they will have to behave if they wish to join everybody else next time.

Do your utmost to avoid punishing an entire group for the sins of a few. For example, it isn't fair to say, 'Since some of you won't be quiet, all of you will sit still until I have total silence.' The children who are quiet should be allowed to go, if that is appropriate, or to move into a quiet group and do something until you have regained control.

In the same way, it is your responsibility to identify wrongdoers. For example, it isn't fair, however desperate you are, to say, 'I want the children who stole all the plants to own up – until they do, the summer picnic is cancelled.' From the children's point of view, most of them are losing out for just being there. Some, maybe most, are also being punished for their ignorance of who actually did the deed; they don't even have the choice of telling.

Physical punishment

Good practice and the law

Guidelines for good practice with the under-8s unanimously recommend that you avoid any form of physical punishment of children. This includes smacking, shoving or shaking children. Many nurseries and centres for children, below and of school age, have a policy of using no physical forms of punishment or persuasion to get children to do what you wish.

The 1986 Education Act made it illegal to use corporal punishment in any state school in England, Wales and Scotland. At the time of writing (1992) this kind of legislation has not been extended to other centres for children or to parents and other carers.

Any adult could be prosecuted for assault on a child if physical forms of discipline were judged to be excessive. The problem, of course, is that even the people who approve of using some physical discipline on children disagree about how much is too much.

The case against physical punishment

Not everybody agrees with banning the physical punishment of children. Adults who claim that it is acceptable to smack children give different reasons. Some propose that hitting, or the caning that used to be legal in schools, is an effective deterrent to children's bad behaviour. Some people argue that smacking doesn't do any harm and they may point to their own childhood as evidence.

We have placed physical punishment in this section on tactics you should avoid because we believe that it should not be used on children. You may need to talk with any parents who disagree. They may be concerned that their children are going to be allowed to run wild. As well as explaining your reasons, be ready to explain how you will handle misbehaviour from children.

To help you, we have summarised the arguments against physical punishment.

It is unacceptable to use physical violence on anybody
British society does not generally approve of smacking, shoving, shaking and hitting other adults to make them do what you want or to settle disagreements. Children are people too, so it is not acceptable to do this to them either.

Smacking gives the message that violence is acceptable
Children who are hit learn that this is the way to make people do what you want and to sort out disagreements. Sooner or later they will also hit back at the adults who use physical punishment against them.

Physical punishment can get seriously out of hand
Anyone who depends on smacking to control children's behaviour has to face the problem of what to do when the first smack doesn't work. An adult may then smack harder and longer. He or she is then in serious danger of losing control, whilst blaming the child for this.

A habit of hitting can reflect an adult's mood, not what the children have done

An adult's decision to smack a child often depends more on how that adult is feeling and the situation in which the child was misbehaving than the actual behaviour. Hitting becomes a habit unless adults believe it is wrong and make efforts to find other ways to handle the children's behaviour, and opportunities to walk away from a confrontation.

Even loving parents have been known to smack their children in sheer exhaustion and frustration. This may be understandable; it doesn't make it right.

Smacking is unreliable in the long run

Adults who claim that smacking did them no harm fail to come up with a convincing argument that it did them any real good.

Children who are smacked do sometimes stop what they are doing. Children who are shoved and shaken are physically unable to continue. However, children often don't see the link between what they have done and the physical punishment meted out by the adult; the hurt and the humiliation blocks the chance that they will change their behaviour. This is especially true when they are hit in public.

Hitting is entirely negative – a message of 'don't' rather than 'do'. The effect is unpredictable since some children are cowed and others may rise to the attacks as a power struggle. It becomes a matter of pride to them that they do not cry and that they have energy left to taunt adults.

For your information

For more information and advice try:

★   Newell, Peter 1989: *Children are People Too – the case against physical punishment* (Approach Ltd). Available from EPOCH – see below.
★   The End Physical Punishment of Children Campaign (EPOCH): 77 Holloway Road, London N7 8JZ (*tel.* 071–700 0627).

Final thoughts

Good practice with the under-8s means the willingness to keep learning. You add to your knowledge and extend your skills. You will undoubtedly be helped in your practice by good equipment and a suitable working environment. However, a lot will still depend on how you actually behave in contact with the children and their parents.

Looking to the future you may find it helpful to gather your thoughts by asking yourself a few questions about how you want to progress now.

Children under 8 years

In what ways would I like to extend my knowledge about children?

- In which areas of knowledge am I confident at the moment?
- Do I need to understand more about the development of particular age groups?
- Could I improve my practice by knowing more about cultural backgrounds different to my own?
- Do I need more knowledge in special areas, for example about children who have disabilities?
- How am I reconciling my own adult perspective with trying to see the world through children's eyes?

Activities with children

In what ways might I plan activities for children that are enjoyable and appropriate to their needs?

- What do I especially enjoy doing with children at the moment?
- What have I learned from this workbook about areas into which I could extend?
- Do I need to add some new ideas for activities? Which ideas could I take from this workbook?
- Would it help if I planned activities more, or in a different way?
- Do I need to review what I do with the children?

Working with families

How do I work with children's families at the moment, and how might this change?

- Would it be helpful to think over the kind of relationship that I have or am aiming to have with parents?
- Do I need more understanding of the role of being a parent? Or being a parent in different circumstances from those that I have experienced?

- Should I be extending my knowledge of cultural traditions different from those I know from my own childhood or raising my own family?
- Am I finding confidence in my own skills alongside respect for parents' experience?

Working with the under-8s and with their families takes energy, patience and ingenuity. It can be very hard work. However, the challenges can also be very satisfying.

In a friendly working relationship with parents, you can share the care of the under-8s. You can offer a lot to the families but, in turn, you will often gain skills and experience for yourself. You can watch children change and grow, knowing that you are able to make a positive contribution to their development.

Appendix 1: NVQs/SVQs

The Care Sector Consortium has developed standards for the competence of workers with children under 8. The full set is available from the National Children's Bureau and is entitled *National Occupational Standards for Working with Young Children and their Families*.

These standards describe what workers should be able to do in order to be competent at their job. They are proposed as National Vocational Qualifications (NVQs) in England, Wales and Northern Ireland, and Scottish Vocational Qualifications (SVQs) in Scotland.

At each level of qualification there is a set of core units; all workers must achieve competence in these. There is a choice of other units which are important for particular kinds of work.

This workbook supports the core units for Level 3; these are listed below. You can see which sections to turn to if you wish to use this book together with the core units.

Level 3 core units	Sections of this book
C.2 Care for children's physical needs	2.5, 3.1, 3.2, 3.4
C.3 Promote the physical development of young children	3.1, 3.2, Ch. 4
C.5 Promote children's social and emotional development	Ch. 1, 3.5, 7.3
C.7 Provide for the management of children's behaviour	5.2, Ch. 7
C.10 Promote children's sensory and intellectual development	1.2, 1.3, Ch. 6
C.11 Promote the development of children's language and communication skills	Ch. 5
C.15 Contribute to the protection of children from abuse	3.3, 3.5
C.16 Observe and assess the development and behaviour of children	2.7, 7.2
E.1 Maintain a child-orientated environment	2.4, 2.5, 2.6
E.2 Maintain the safety of children	2.5, 3.3, 3.4
P.2 Establish and maintain relationships with parents of young children	1.1, 2.4

Appendix 2:
How to find out more

Throughout the workbook we have suggested organisations who may be able to help you on specific issues in care of the under-8s.

What follows is a list of organisations that may be helpful in a more general way. Please see this list as a beginning and add to it yourself. Many of the publications suggested in the workbook and in Appendix 3 also have lists of addresses.

VOLCUF and the Early Childhood Unit (see addresses below) have compiled a national directory (1992): *Organisations Concerned with Young Children and their Families.*

Access to Information on Multi-cultural Education Resources (AIMER)
Faculty of Education and Community
   Studies
University of Reading
Bulmershe Court
Earley
Reading RG6 1HY

tel. 0734 875123 ext. 4870/1

Action for Sick Children
Argyle House
29–31 Euston Road
London NW1 2SD

tel. 071–833 2041

The organisation used to be known as the National Association for the Welfare of Children in Hospital (NAWCH).

Advisory Centre for Education
18 Victoria Park Square
London E2 9PB

tel. 081–980 4596

Afro-Caribbean Education Resource Centre
ACER Centre
Wyvil Road
London SW8 2TJ

tel. 071–627 2662

Child Accident Prevention Trust
18–20 Farringdon Lane
EC1R 3AU

tel. 071–608 3828

Comhairle Nan Sgoiltean Araich (The Gaelic Pre-School Council)
21a Castle Street
Inverness IV2 3ER

tel. 0463 225469

Council for Disabled Children
8 Wakley Street
London EC1V 7QE

tel. 071–278 9441

Previously known as the Voluntary Council for Handicapped Children.

Children's Legal Centre
20 Compton Terrace
London N1 2UN

tel. 071–359 6251

Commission for Racial Equality
Elliot House
10–12 Allington Street
London SW1E 5EH

tel. 071–828 7022

Development Education Centre
Selly Oak Colleges
Bristol Road
Birmingham B29 6LE

tel. 021–472 3255

Early Childhood Unit
8 Wakley Street
London EC1V 7QE

tel. 071–278 9441

The Unit is part of the National
Children's Bureau.

Early Years Trainers' Anti-Racist
Network (EYTARN)
The Lyndens
51 Granville Road
London N12 0JH

tel. 081–446 7056

Health Education Authority
78 New Oxford Street
London WC1 1AH

tel. 071–631 6930

Kids' Club Network
279–281 Whitechapel Road
London E1 1BY

tel. 071–247 3009

The network used to be called the
National Out-of-School Alliance.

Mudiad Ysgolion Meithrin (Association
of Welsh Pre-School Playgroups)
10 Grove Park
Cardiff CF1 3BN
Wales

tel. 0222 485510

National Association for Gifted Children
1 South Audley Street
London W1Y 5DQ

tel. 071–499 1188

National Association for the Welfare of
Children in Hospital (NAWCH)
– see Action for Sick Children.

National Childminding Association
(NCMA)
8 Masons Hill
Bromley
BR2 9EY

tel. 081–464 6164/460 5427

National Children's Bureau (NCB)
8 Wakley Street
London EC1V 7QE

tel. 071–278 9441

National Children's Play and Recreation
Unit
356–361 Euston Road
London NW1 3AL

tel. 071–383 5455

National Out-of-School Alliance
– see Kids' Club Network.

National Stepfamily Association
72 Willesden Lane
London NW6 7TA

tel. office 071–372 0844; counselling
service: 071–372 0846

National Voluntary Council for
Children's Play
8 Wakley Street
London EC1V 7QE

tel. 071–278 9441

Plant yng Nghymru (Children in Wales)
7 Cleeve House
Lambourne Crescent
Cardiff CF4 5GJ

tel. 0222 761177

Playboard Northern Ireland
253 Lisburn Road
Belfast BT9 7EN

tel. 0232 382633

Pre-school Playgroups Association
61–63 Kings Cross Road
London WC1X 9LL

tel. 071–833 0991

Scottish Out-of-School Alliance
c/o Strathclyde After-School Care
Association
39 Hope Street, Glasgow G2 6AE

tel. 041–221 8119

Thomas Coram Research Unit
27–28 Woburn Square
London WC1H 0AA

tel. 071–612 6957

Voluntary Council for Handicapped
Children
– see Council for Disabled Children.

Voluntary Organisations Liaison Council
for the Under-Fives (VOLCUF)
77 Holloway Road
London N7 8JZ

tel. 071–607 9573

Working Group Against Racism in
Children's Resources (WGARCR)
Lady Margaret Hall Settlement
460 Wandsworth Road
London SW8 3LX

tel. 071–627 4594

Appendix 3:
Useful books and articles

Publications

Many publications are suggested throughout the workbook. You may find these books helpful also.

Campion, Jean 1991: *Counselling Children* (Whiting & Birch).
Dreikurs, Rudolf 1972: *Happy Children* (Fontana).
Dunn, Judy 1984: *Sisters and Brothers* (Fontana).
Elliott, Claire 1992: *Childhood* (Channel Four Television).
Epstein, Debbie and Alison Sealey 1990: *Where it Really Matters – developing anti-racist education in predominantly white primary schools* (Development Education Centre).
Herbert, Martin 1988: *Working with Children and their Families* (Routledge).
Howe, Michael 1990: *Sense and Nonsense about Hothouse Children – a practical guide for parents and teachers* (British Psychological Society).
Jolly, June 1981: *The Other Side of Paediatrics: a guide to everyday care of sick children* (Macmillan).
Lindon, Jennie and Lance 1993: *Your Child From 5–11* (Hodder & Stoughton).
Miedzian, Myriam 1992: *Boys will be Boys – breaking the link between masculinity and violence* (Virago).
Milner, David 1983: *Children and Race – ten years on* (Ward Lock Educational).
Murgatroyd, Stephen 1985: *Counselling and Helping* (Methuen).
Oaklander, Violet 1978: *Windows on Our Children* (Real People Press).
Pugh, Gillian (ed.) 1992: *Contemporary Issues in the Early Years* (Paul Chapman/NCB).
Rudolph Schaffer, H. 1990: *Making Decisions about Children – psychological questions and answers* (Basil Blackwell).
Smith, Peter K. and Helen Cowrie 1988: *Understanding Children's Development*, 2nd edn (Basil Blackwell).
Tizard, Barbara and others 1988: *Young Children at School in the Inner City* (Laurence Erlbaum Associates).

To help you choose books and toys

Depending on where you work, you may it hard to find some of the books and play materials that you would like. You could try two large manufacturers – Galts and Nottingham Educational Supplies – both of whom offer good-quality play materials.

Two shops have been very helpful to us over the years, especially in our search for books and toys appropriate for a multicultural Britain. At the time of writing, neither of them runs a mail-order service as such, but like any good shop will get you books or play resources if you know what you want:

- Bookspread: 58 Tooting Bec Road, London SW17 8BE (*tel.* 081–767 6377/4551).
- Childsplay: 112 Tooting High Street, London SW17 0RR (*tel.* 081–672 6470).

The WGARCR has a useful review, *Guidelines for the Evaluation and Selection of Toys and Other Resources for Children*, which also gives some addresses for large and smaller suppliers.

The children's book magazine *Books for Keeps* is a valuable source of information on publications. This could be especially helpful if you do not have a good bookshop close to you or have very little time for browsing. The publishers also produce special guides to publications; they have, for example, guides on books for a multicultural society, on poetry for children, and books with an environmental theme.

- *Books for Keeps*: 6 Brightfield Road, Lee, London SE12 8QF (*tel.* 081–852 4953).

Index

abuse of children, 56, 65–6, 82–5
AIDS, 57, 78–9
assessment, *see* observation
asthma, 76

babies
  care of, 56–7, 67, 68
  cot death, 57–8
behaviour
  adults', 143, 145–8, 155–60
  children's, 82–4, 142–4
  consequences of, 152–4
  observation of, 49–52, 145–7
  positive handling of children's, 152–4
  talking with children about, 148
books for children
  choosing and using, 111–12
  on particular topics: craft ideas, 100;
    disabilities, 75, 118; families and
    life events, 82, 138, 139, 140; food,
    63; illness, 75; in different
    languages, 110–11; religion, 141;
    safety, 66; sciences, 137;
    storytelling, 113

care
  children learning own care, 65–72
  of sick children, 73–4
  importance of, 19, 55
childhood
  in general, 1–4
  workers' own, 4, 13, 21, 69
children, *see also* development
  abuse of, 82–5
  behaviour of, 16, 30, 82–4, 142–4
  feelings, *see* emotions
  in distress, 81–5
  individuality of, 12–17, 24, 157
  names of, 13
  needs of, 5–7
  who are ill, 73–80
  with disabilities, *see* special needs
Children Act 1989, *vii*, 22
communication
  bilingual children, 109–10, 122
  body language, 101–2, 104, 143
  concerns about, 115–16
  development, 102–6

disabilities and, 116–18
use of language, 105
with babies and children, 53–4, 55–6,
  74–5, 81, 107–9, 147–8, 149
with children in a group, 13, 113–15
with co-workers, 20, 53, 84, 150, 151,
  152, 155
with parents, 28–30, 31, 53–4, 81,
  151–2
confidentiality, 27, 51, 84
cultural and racial differences, 1, 7, 12,
  19, 21, 59, 62–3, 69, 71, 83, 102,
  140

development
  as individuals, 12–17
  experiences, 2, 3, 81
  learning self-care, 65–71
  observation and, 47–9
  of communication and language, 101–
    6
  of thinking, 92, 125–9
  physical, 86–93
  theories of, 8–11
diet
  allergies, 64
  different diets, 59–60
  drink, 60, 71
  healthy, 59–64
  religious considerations, 63
disabilities, *see* special needs
dyslexia, 123–4

eczema, 76
Education Act 1981, 54
Education Reform Act 1988, 54
emotions, children's
  expressing and understanding, 15, 16,
    139, 143
  illness and, 74–5
  needs, 5–6, 143
encouragement of children, 6, 16, 38,
  41, 52, 66–7, 69–79, 99, 130, 152–3
environment
  creating a positive, 15, 16–17, 34–8
  impact of, 2, 3, 9–10
epilepsy, 77–8
equal opportunities
  explanation of, 24–6

families 3, 12, 83, 138–9
feeding babies and children, 4, 68–9
feelings, *see* emotions
fits, 77–8
food, *see* diet

good practice
  and the law, 22–3, 54, 159
  principles and, 18–21

hay fever, 76
head lice, 79
hearing loss, 117–18
HIV, 78–9; *see also* AIDS

ideas, children learning
  attitudes, 3, 105, 126–9
  colours, 127–8, 130–1
  distance, 136–7
  measurement, 128
  numbers and maths, 128, 131–3
  relationships and growing up, 43,
    128, 138–40
  sciences, 128, 137
  shape and size, 134–6
  speed, 136–7
  time, 128, 133–4
intellectual development, 10, 125–7; *see
  also* ideas
intellectual needs, 6

language, *see* communication
learning, 8, 9, 40–1, 130, 141–4, 145

National Curriculum, 40, 43, 54
National Vocational Qualifications
  (NVQs/SVQs), *vii*, 163

observation
  approach and methods, 47–52, 99,
    145–7
  by children, 141–2
  objectivity and, 29, 46
  sharing with children, 53–4
  sharing with parents, 29, 53
  writing up, 50–1

parents
  communication with, 27–30, 51–2, 60,
    62, 65
  confidentiality and access to files, 51
  contract with, 27–8
  meaning of partnership with, 20, 27,
    30
  ways of involving, 31–2, 51
physical
  development, 65–72
  games, 95–6
  needs of children, 5
play, 6–7
play activities
  cooking, 67, 132
  creative and craft work, 97–9
  dance, 97
  for exploring ideas, 130–41
  games, 95–6
  helping out as play, 37–8, 66–7
  materials, 42–3
  music, 97

planning and evaluating, 41–2
prejudice
  children learning, 2, 3, 24, 151
  discrimination, racial, 23
  offensive remarks, 150–2
Race Relations Act 1976, 23
reading, children learning, 119–21
records and reports
  for own learning, *viii*
  on children and families, 32, 50–1, 84
religious beliefs
  children and, 140
  diet and, 63
rules for children, 149–54

safety
  cleanliness and sterilisation, 56–7, 80
  general, 35–7
  teaching children about, 65–6, 126
settling children, 31
sickle-cell disease, 77
sleep and rest, 57–8

smacking, 30, 159–60
special needs, 6, 55, 70, 74–5, 90, 92–3,
    99, 109, 116–18, 123–4

temperament, 14–18
thalassaemia, 77
threadworms, 79–80
toilet-training, 4, 69–70
touch
  children's need for, 55–6
  inappropriate, 56, 82–3

workers
  attitudes and expectations, 4, 25–6,
    44–6, 59, 71–2
  behaviour towards children, 107–9
  behaviour towards parents, 27–33
  definition of term, *viii*
  own experiences and skills, 4, 13, 19,
    20, 21, 25, 33, 69, 161–2
  ratio of workers to children, 37
  values, 30
writing, children learning, 121–3